Bounce!

Bounce!

Failure, Resiliency, and Confidence to Achieve Your Next Great Success

BARRY J. MOLTZ

WILEY

John Wiley & Sons, Inc.

Published by John Wiley & Sons, Inc., Hoboken, New Jersey.
Published simultaneously in Canada.

For general information on our other products and services or for technical support, please
contact our Customer Care Department within the United States at (800) 762-2974, outside
the United States at (317) 572-3993 or fax (317) 572-4002.

Wiley also publishes its books in a variety of electronic formats. Some content that appears in
print may not be available in electronic books. For more information about Wiley products,
visit our web site at www.wiley.com.

Library of Congress Cataloging-in-Publication Data:

Moltz, Barry J.
    Bounce! : failure, resiliency, and confidence to achieve your next great success / Barry J. Moltz.
        p.   cm.
    Includes bibliographical references and index.
    ISBN 978-0-470-22408-3 (cloth)
        1. Success in business.   2. Business failures.   3. Success.   I. Title.
    HF5386.M735 2008
    650.1—dc22

                                                                        2007028894

Printed in the United States of America

10   9   8   7   6   5   4   3   2   1

To my wife, Sara,
who has shown me
that body and mind
truly are connected.

To my sons,
who teach me every day
what bounce really is.

Stand like a mountain.

—Jun Shihan Nancy Lanoue,
Thousand Waves Seido Karate

There is a mountain in you. Please get in touch with it.
You are more solid and resilient than you think.

—Thich Nhat Hanh,
Vietnamese Zen Buddhist monk

I just want to go out and drive.
And no matter what happened,
my children and lady will love me.

—Ricky Bobby in Talladega Nights:
The Ballad of Ricky Bobby

Contents

Preface

When I was writing my first book, I came to terms with my own personal brand of craziness to realize that crazy isn't always such a bad thing. Over the past five years since *You Need to Be a Little Crazy* (Kaplan Business, 2003) hit the shelves, tens of thousands of people have either read the book or come to hear me speak. They tell me that they don't think my brand of crazy is all bad. In fact, I get questions all the time about how I learned to make it through the crazy ups and downs of business with such bounce, and can I help others figure out how to do it, too?

So that's what I set out to accomplish with this book. The product of my 25 years of experience in business, *Bounce!* is about developing confidence—and not just any sort of confidence. This is a book about developing bounce, a kind of true business confidence that brings its own special brand of resiliency.

But this is not a book about coming back from failure.

Comeback books have been written many times before. The comeback is romanticized in society and totally overrated. This is a book about accepting failure as a normal part of the process, even when there isn't something to learn. Failure that offers no real learning value jolts the business belief system. It is time for people to start telling their stories about *those* failures, which visit us all, without the redemption of any subsequent successes.

That's how quantitative research always begins—with people telling their stories. Then someone starts writing those stories down. Another person begins to collect data to support or rebut; someone else creates a model, and then the body of predictive results begins to build. But it all begins with people talking.

This book is a blend of personal experiences, famous people's stories, and firsthand interviews with people who aren't famous yet. You will read about well-known people, but more importantly, you will share in the experiences and insights of other businesspeople you have never heard of and probably will never meet. (Mini biographies of the not-so-famous are at the back of the book.) These people have entrusted me to retell their tales so that we all may learn from them. People like these live with you and me under the bell-shaped curve where most of life happens for many of us.

This book is about bounce: the process of bounding back, of moving forward, falling back, and shooting ahead again, and through all that, building up and then drawing on personal reserves of energy. I describe ten *building bands*—beliefs, tools, and processes that every businessperson can use to develop true business confidence built on resiliency and bounce. You grab these things along the way in your business and life experiences. This book will help you consciously recognize the things that can give you bounce.

When we possess bounce, we are able to move forward from any event, situation, or outcome—good or bad—to the next place where a decision can be made based on the choices currently available to us. We develop the best process we can and then make a clear decision.

Bounce allows us to be passionately excited and intensely enthusiastic about our businesses and our lives. Above all, bounce gets us ready for adventure. Of all the wild places I have been in the world, from New York to New Zealand, there is never a ride that can compare to the one that business can provide.

Acknowledgments

Many authors say that the second book is the most difficult of their career to write. The popular quip goes that you have your whole life to write the first book but only three years to write the second one. For any artist, the second work is a difficult one. Unfortunately, I've proven that adage once again. It has taken me four years to write this book. I want to thank the following people.

Katherine Stoica read countless books and did many interviews as research for the book. She probably knows more stories right now about failure and other seemingly useless information than any other chemistry major. She has been an incredibly valuable marketing assistant for me over the past few years.

Mary Jane Grinstead was my mentor 25 years ago when I started IBM two weeks after I graduated college. When I was 21, I wanted to be just like her. She reincarnated herself about seven years ago as an author and journalist. I have been fortunate to reconnect and collaborate with her as she edited this book. Amazing as it seems, Mary Jane was able to take my ramblings and rants and place them into a cohesive context. She consistently asked me, "What do you believe?" It has been one of the most gratifying parts of writing this second book—to reignite the business passion that burns inside both of us.

Marshall, Russ, Alan, Jen, and Daryl at Eslide, a graphic design company that specializes in professional quality presentations, were able to translate my scribbles into effective illustrations. Their extreme customer support is world class!

Jill Kickul, professor at Miami University of Ohio, had her students provide research and interview international businesses that are included in the book.

Kat Zwicka continues to be my massage therapist in times of needs. She reconnects my mind with my body the best she can.

Heidi Milby, my first Pilates trainer, tells me I am the most inflexible man she has ever met. This is one thing that my wife and business associates agree on. Motion is lotion! **Annette Gryniewicz,** my second Pilates trainer keeps telling me to stop thinking and do it. She sees value in action too.

Ali "Farka" Touré is the only musician I could listen to when I wrote this book. Although I had no idea what he was singing about, Touré's brand of African world music put me in whatever state of mind I needed to be in to put these words on paper. I never met the Malian singer and musician; he died in 2006 at the age of 66.

Jun Shihan Nancy Lanoue and Kyoshi Sarah Ludden, my Seido Karate teachers at Thousand Waves, teach me the meaning of confidently striving with patience. As a result, I have been able to do things I never thought possible. Deep bow and osu.

Matt, Shannon, Christine, and Jessica at Wiley & Sons helped shape this manuscript into a book.

Paige Wheeler at Folio Literary Management always laughed with me when I would call her while I was in Los Angeles and say, "Hey, I am in L.A. on the phone with my agent!"

My parents, **Alan and Carole,** tricked me into thinking I could accomplish almost anything I set my mind to. It worked.

Mike Cooper, my father-in-law, may he rest in peace, was surely one cool business cat. He exemplified true business confidence to me and definitely had the bounce of nine lives.

Finally, in the past few years, I have traveled around the world speaking to thousands of businesspeople at hundreds of business events. During and after the events, we laugh and sometimes cry together as they ask questions. What has surprised me the most has been people's willingness to share their experiences, both good and bad. What has impressed me the most is what they taught me in the process. I want to thank them, too, for participating in this book.

CHAPTER 1

Get Ready for Adventure: You Have Never Heard a Speaker Like This Before

I am an entrepreneur and business owner who has been a keynote speaker at more than 100 business events. The biography that I provide to the event organizers for my introduction always begins like this:

> Barry has been starting and running businesses for 15 years with a great deal of success *and failure*.

I wrote my introduction this way specifically to drive home that I am different from most of the other business speakers that my hosts and audiences have hired or heard before. While most if not all of us have failed more than once in our business careers, we prefer not to discuss our failures. I talk about my failures—honestly, openly, and often from the stage.

Many times the person who actually makes the introduction will skip over the "*and failure*" part, thinking it must be an error or possibly a deliberate joke by me or by the event organizers to trip them up or get a laugh. Alternately, they sometimes say "*and failure*" quite awkwardly, especially if they haven't reviewed the script of my introduction ahead of time.

Most people who speak publicly provide an endless litany of their achievements. Why on earth would a celebrated keynote speaker want to reveal that along with his success, he has also experienced so much failure? Certainly, this speaker—this Barry Moltz, whom we hired to inspire and educate us with his wonderful success stories and anecdotes—does not truly intend for his eager audience to know that he's failed at anything.

Invariably, if the audience is listening, my success/failure introduction will get a little chuckle or maybe even a nervous laugh. However, within a few minutes after I've expanded a bit on my failures—talking about how many of them were hard stops, dead ends, failures that didn't lead to either success, a comeback story, a happy ending, or even a lesson learned—I can see on many of the faces in the audience that they are thinking, "Wow, this guy and I have something in common. I have had both success *and* failure in my life. I can definitely relate." With this realization, my audience is more able and ready to listen and to learn from what I have to say.

When I discuss my past failures, my listeners' brightening eyes and half-smiles signal their very first thought, which is likely not one of empathy, but of relief. I can almost read their minds as they tell themselves, "Thank you, Lord, that it happened to him and not to me." Some of you reading this book, much like my face-to-face audiences, may have had this feeling more than once.

Eventually someone in the audience poses the question: "Barry, how did you survive all that?" They want to learn the magic trick to ride through their next difficult situation and come out the other end, too.

Talk the Talk

We businesspeople all love to talk about our successes, and why not? They remind us of the times that we stared down a particular business situation and won. These are the times when we arm-wrestled the bad guys (our competitors) and pinned them to the ground. These are the times our success offered a path to living happily ever after (at a financial profit).

For a long time, whenever I succeeded at something, I felt fulfilled because that was exactly the promised outcome of the archetypal stories of success that my parents drilled into me when I was young—and if you had parents who wanted to direct and motivate you into having what they saw as a good life, you know the stories I'm talking about.

My mother told me that when I grew up, life would be nothing short of a magic carpet ride. If I worked hard, every year I would advance in my career, be recognized for my accomplishments, and earn more money.

In our formative years, we need this encouraging picture of the future, but as we gain experience, we realize that life and business do not always work out this way. Reality has a way of colliding with our parents' dream scenarios and our own carefully constructed plans.

The Ultimate Reality Show

This collision is not a bad thing; it is just a part of daily business life. Many times we encounter less-than-perfect results that we wish could have worked out differently. Other times, we end up with a result so far from perfect that it can only be described as ugly, painful, and debilitating. Paint it with broad strokes in any color you want, but *failure* is the only word that accurately describes situations like these.

When we do fail, conventional business wisdom comforts us, saying that failure is a good thing because it teaches so much. We are continually reminded by those around us that failure is an important ingredient in the next success, possibly even a prerequisite. Sometimes we listen to this soothing mantra because in our tattered state, it consoles us. We tell ourselves that failure "happened to us" so that we could learn some important lesson that would later propel us to even greater success.

This stream of logic might make us feel good, but if failure is truly a critical component of success, why are so many of us unwilling to talk about our disasters as openly as we talk about our successes? Why can't friends and associates help us figure out all the important things we are supposed to learn from screwing up? We give lip service to the benefits of failure when it's happening to someone else; but when it's our turn in the crosshairs, we clam up.

Here's one thing I know: People love it when I speak about my failures. As I tell my tales of how I went out of business, I see it in their eyes. They love to hear about how my partners kicked me out of our company. They are mesmerized when I tell them that I thought I was going blind before I actually came down with diabetes. They can't wait to hear the next part of my tale when I say that after I was diagnosed with diabetes I fell into a depression that included panic attacks and anorexia—that I was days away from checking into a mental health facility.

The television networks understand this human trait very well. They know their viewers are riveted to the calamities covered in the news as long as it is about someone else. Remember watching the victims of Hurricane Katrina clinging to their rooftops, or eavesdropping on the collective misery inside the Superdome? This fascination is also the reason for the popularity of reality television shows all over the world.

While there are many differences in cultural attitudes toward failure or tragedy, as we see later in this book, most people share this common trait: Seeing other people going through failure helps us see our own situation in a more positive light. It isn't that we aren't empathetic, but we do feel better that it's not us. Seeing someone who is worse off than we are raises our spirits, not necessarily in a malevolent way, but so that we can recognize that things may not be as bad as they seem, and certainly they could be much worse.

In his book *The Pursuit of Happiness* (Harper, 1993), David Myers says, "Happiness is relative not only to our past experience but also to our comparisons with others. We are always comparing ourselves with others. And whether we feel good or bad depends on who those others are. We are slow-witted or clumsy only when others are smart or agile."[1]

The Comeback: See, Dreams Can Come True

Businesspeople like hearing tales of failure that are followed by a big comeback story as much or even more than they like hearing stories of tragedy. Remember Sylvester Stallone as Rocky Balboa in his famous 1976 movie, *Rocky*. He came to symbolize the underdog who wins. In 2006, Rocky even came out of retirement (he now owns a restaurant!) for one last shot at regaining the boxing title, and people flocked to the theaters to cheer him on.

In fact, in this country, we love the underdog so much that in the late 1960s and early 1970s there was an American cartoon series about a crime-fighting superhero called Underdog. The character, who completely personified the unlikely superhero, was a small beagle with flesh-colored fur, a big, black nose, and oversized, floppy ears. Underdog got his strength from a super vitamin pill that he kept in a compartment on his ring.[2] There are many times (especially before I begin a speech) that I've wished I owned one of those rings!

At some level, we all recognize that we are or have been an underdog; we want the hope that someday we, too, will swirl a satin cape and be the winner.

I have had my own personal comeback. At the second company I started, I learned how important teammates are to the overall success of a company when my business partners kicked me off the team. I had chosen to start a company with partners I had found in the classified section of a local newspaper. This was not my smartest move. When I started my third business, I didn't make the same mistake. I knew my partner well and valued him and our other team members far more than I valued the business itself. I did learn from a past experience in order to come back and achieve a better outcome.

There are many times that failure teaches lessons that we might not be able to learn another way; but there are also plenty of times when there is nothing (or almost nothing) new to be learned from failure. There are times when dead-end failure just plain stinks, and you can't pretty it up or minimize the pain by ferreting out something of value from the mess.

My third company once lost its largest customer because the U.S. Securities and Exchange Commission (SEC) caught them stealing. Another time, I lost my best employee because her spouse took a new job 1,000 miles away. There wasn't much new for me to learn from either of these situations that I didn't already know. I already knew not to do business with criminals, and I knew that I would keep on hiring good people no matter whether their spouses had the potential to be transferred or not. However, since it's not possible (short of hiring spies or engaging in other invasive practices) to know what goes on inside other companies or to know our employees' personal goals until they choose to share them, there was nothing in either of these situations that I could have done differently.

Incidents like these just happen; they are examples of a kind of inevitability that exists in business cycles. There are times of success, and there will be offsetting times of failure. Many things can create failure—*create,* not *cause:* a person's actions, the actions of others, the external environment, or perhaps the phases of the moon.

There are steps you can take to help you experience and endure those knocked-on-your-rear effects of failure differently. My goal is to help you learn how to turn these painful experiences into "aha!" moments and develop a business confidence that will be the foundation of your own personal brand of business success.

To increase business confidence, we need to be comfortable with the uncomfortable. We need to be at ease with not knowing what is going to come next, and with knowing that we are never going to know all that we don't know. This is hard to accept for businesspeople who are always trying to predict the future with formulaic precision, when the truth is that it's impossible to know what will come next.

A Messy Process

Gaining true business confidence by bouncing is messy. Bouncing is not an exact process. When a process is created, it is mostly through trial and error. You can't get it right by just riding your success or just learning lessons from failing. How do you structure a process for something that generally isn't repeatable? There are so many ever-changing variables that contribute to any outcome in business that a rote methodology is impossible to structure. Therefore, telling you to take action A in situation B will only help you in situation B. It won't matter a speck in situation B-2, or in C through Z, or all the rest.

To develop a sense of ease, we must come to the personal realization that we can survive almost any outcome, despite how treacherous it may be. Beyond that, we must learn how to look forward to what will come (genuinely rather than with false bravado) because we have the confidence that we will be okay no matter what.

Armed with this knowledge, we will resist judging events as failures or successes. We will see them only as opportunities to make a decision that will eventually move us toward an outcome that we want, if the current result is not, to our way of thinking, optimal.

To accomplish this shift in my own life, I needed tools that I didn't have. These weren't the tools we learned about at business school, or the tools we develop through business training as I did in my early career at IBM. I'm talking about tools of an entirely different sort.

When I was young, I used to make rubber band balls. I started by covering a tissue with rubber bands—from my newspaper route, from the grocery store, and from my father's office drawers. Once my rubber band ball got as big as a baseball, I bounced it—against the side of the house, my mother's car, the street in front of our house, my sister's head.[3]

Building true business confidence is a lot like making a rubber band ball. Put together bit by bit, the elastic bands give the ball bounce. Like experiences, rubber bands come in many different shapes and colors. They stretch in different directions, and they have many diverse uses. Rubber bands rarely break, but when they do snap, they sting, though only for a short period of time.

Like building true business confidence, building a rubber band ball is a project that is never complete. Some bands fray over time and need to be replaced. As rubber bands are added, the ball with its random orientation will never bounce the same way twice.

In the business journey, there are tools and skills that we can develop. The tools I'm talking about don't come about or fit together in a predictable, linear manner; they don't stack or square up like building blocks. Instead, developing true business confidence and resiliency comes about more in the winding, uncharted way of building a rubber band ball.

The path that I outline to business confidence and resiliency comes about by snapping or layering on ten *building bands.* Think of it as building a rubber band ball that will give you the bounce to develop resiliency for true business confidence.

The process begins by forgetting the tenets of business we thought were true.

CHAPTER 2

Archetypes of Success: Be Careful What You Wish For

For a long time, I thought that the Greeks had it right. In their mythology, Dionysus, the god of fertility and wine, offered King Midas a reward in recognition of his hospitality toward Silenus, Dionysus' schoolmaster. Midas, a great seeker of wealth, boldly replied, "I want everything I touch to turn to gold," and Dionysus granted his wish.

After that, everything Midas touched turned to gold—including food and drink. Even his lovely young daughter was turned into a golden statue. Thus did Midas's wish become more of a curse than a gift. To rid himself of this power so he could relieve his starvation and get his daughter back alive, King Midas prayed to Dionysus again. He was told to wash in the river Pactolus. Midas did, and the power passed to the river, whose sands turned to gold.

Today, we admiringly refer to people who seem to make money at everything they do as having the "Midas touch." This has a very favorable connotation and is something that many businesspeople strive to achieve. Why? We offer many reasons—to have a better life and to better provide for the family; to be honored, respected, and looked up to; and to be happy. In our minds, we walk around with one formula in our head:

$$Money = Success = Happiness$$

Indeed, money is often the measure of success in business, but think about the mathematical properties of this relationship. If the equation were accurate, you could drop any one of the elements and the other two would still equal each other—which is likely impossible in life, and yet this is often a deeply rooted belief of businesspeople.

During the past 25 years, as I moved through my own personal and business cycles of failure and success (never in the linear path or the balanced relationship that this formula suggests), I have met plenty of people who I am certain would seriously consider giving up food, drink, and maybe even their mother-in-law for a month of the Midas touch. I know for sure that there are some days when I wish I could turn my sons into gold statues for at least an hour or two.

From childhood, we grow up wishing, working, and hoping for huge financial success because we think this will lead to happiness. Financial wealth and the notion of success are closely linked in everything we listen to, read, and learn; this cause-and-effect relationship fills our business magazines and our daily news.

We tend to respect and even revere those who have become rich; we set them up as modern-day heroes and gods. There is a great Yiddish proverb that goes, "With money in your pocket, you are wise, you are handsome, and you sing well, too."[1] Many of us grew up in households where we were taught that "Money isn't everything— but it's a long way ahead of what comes next,"[2] and too many of us are teaching our children the same thing. That's because this premise sounds reasonable and logical. It's one of those statements that's hard to rebut. Similarly, Midas thought having a golden touch would make him supremely happy, and look how wrong he was.

Studies suggest that many of us, like Midas, think that money can buy happiness, and we hold to that belief until something teaches us otherwise. Consider the findings of psychologists Brickman, Coates, and Janoff-Bulman:

> The researchers studied both lottery winners and individuals that sustained a physical injury, to determine if winning the lottery made them happier or if sustaining an injury made them less happy. What they found was that immediately after either event, levels of happiness were higher (lottery winners), or lower (physically injured), and that after eight weeks or less, people returned to the level of happiness they had before the event. This research suggests that we adapt to these situations very quickly, and often return to the degree of happiness we had before such an event.[3]

So if happiness is a state that isn't permanently influenced up or down by something as financially huge as winning the lottery or as painful as sustaining a personal injury, maybe we are mistaken in thinking that wealth, success, and happiness are related—and in attributing such stature to those who make it big.

In a speech I heard delivered in 2006, small business expert Steven S. Little commented that we choose most of our heroes based not on their wealth accumulation but on something else.[4] Little says that we remember our heroes for their effort, their values, or their ideas. We don't remember how much money they made. We remember the steps they took to get there—the process they followed, their trials and tribulations, and how they reacted to those—and not the financial outcome that might have followed.

Applying Little's analysis to the earlier example, do we remember Midas because he had the golden touch or because of the failure brought about by that golden touch? We remember him because of what he learned and how his definition of happiness and success changed as he realized that his daughter was literally worth more than gold.

And yet, despite studies, myths, anecdotes, and, yes, even books suggesting otherwise, many of us hold on to the idea that if we were just given the chance, money would buy us happiness, respect, and acclaim. Research studies and thoughtful advice are no match for pop culture and urban legends in which many of the most financially successful businesspeople are actors, rock stars, sports idols, and enormously compensated CEOs.

Often we reverence these icons regardless of the methods they used to accumulate their wealth or what kind of character they may have. We read their books (often badly ghost-written) and flock to seminars where we hope to learn the secrets of how the rich get rich because we want to be rich, too. One of the financial bibles of our time is Robert Kyosaki's best seller *Rich Dad, Poor Dad: What the Rich Teach Their Kids about Money—That the Poor and Middle Class Do Not!* (Warner Books, 2000). The very title of this book attracts readers by suggesting that we can get in on the secrets of the rich and teach them to our children.

Archetype One: Making Something from Nothing or At Least Not Much

There are three pervasive archetypal models[5] for achieving success. We are taught that following any one of these leads to financial success which then sets us up to live the happiness dream. Every goal needs a measurement system, and since money is seen as the source of success and happiness, we are taught to measure our business success (and many times our value in life) by how much money we make. Alternately, our failure can also be measured by how much money we do *not* earn.

Most people have heard the story of Bill Gates, the Harvard University dropout who founded Microsoft and became one of the world's richest men. You probably also know about the rise of Michael Dell, who founded his company in his University of Texas dorm room and left college to start PCs Limited (later renamed the Dell Corporation).

All something-from-nothing stories share similar characteristics. An unknown person lacking in financial resources starts with an idea and works hard. They get a bit of luck, work harder still for a few years, and *boom!* Their linear road to financial success (represented in Figure 2.1) yields millions of dollars; they have now achieved the American dream, and they have attained a sort of mythical stature in society.

This is not surprising given the immigrant nature of America. Jonathan Black writes in *Yes You Can!* (Bloomsbury, 2006) that "our country was founded on the belief that something better lay over the horizon. Those early souls braved months at sea, storms, illness, death to improve their lot. America was the land of opportunity . . . you could start with nothing and end up with something."[6]

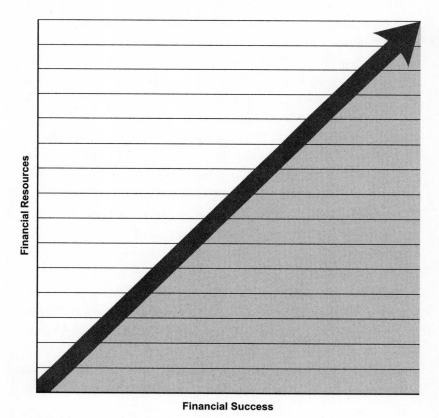

FIGURE 2.1 Archetype One: Something from Not Much

As businesspeople, we love something-from-nothing stories because we can easily imagine ourselves coming from limited resources and achieving the spectacular financial success our parents and teachers taught us to dream of and pursue.

We reason that "if it happened for Michael Dell, it can happen for me." We believe that we are smarter and can work harder than the average person. Business books are traditionally filled with stories that inspire us to work smart and hard to achieve our financial goals, promoting the belief that no matter what our starting point is, we can succeed. The message of this archetype is: If all these other people who didn't start out with the advantages of wealth, position, or family support can do it by relying on their own intelligence, drive, and accomplishments, so can I.

This "work hard" archetype rests on the myth of infinite possibility—that no matter where you start out, you have the potential to be whatever you work to be. Not that you will achieve it, but that the *possibility* is always there. This is probably why most business school students say they want to be entrepreneurs. Since they are spending between $80,000 and $120,000 (not including lost earnings) on an advanced degree, they need to find the quickest path to pay off their college loans and fulfill their financial dreams.

Now comes the cold water: There are times, lots of them, when the myth of infinite possibilities turns out to be just that—a myth. Consider that upon graduation, more than 80 percent of business school graduates seek employment in an established company; they don't start out on their own.[7] They are willing to work hard and long, but the reality of starting a business becomes too difficult and their financial obligations become too great, so they opt instead for working inside an established company.

Once settled on this path, many never start their own business. Is this because they find enough success and fulfillment at their chosen profession, or is it because their fear of failure blocks them from the path they were meant to take? Interestingly, some of the reasons MBA graduates offer when they do reengage their entrepreneurial dreams are that they have been fired, they have created enough security to take the risk, or they are simply too bored to keep doing what they currently do.

Archetype Two: The Rich Get Richer

In this archetype, the businessperson starts with a lot of money and ends up with even more money (as represented in Figure 2.2). It is also the origin of the business cliché, "It takes money to make money," and provides the punch line to a great joke in the business world:

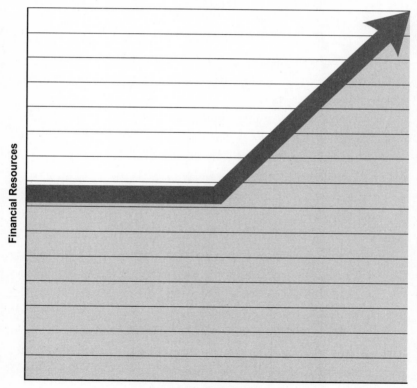

Financial Success

FIGURE 2.2 Archetype Two: The Rich Get Richer

Question: How do you make $100 million?

Answer: Start with $10 million!

This is the Donald Trump archetype. Trump got started with a lot of help from his real estate mogul father, Fred Trump. After studying at the University of Pennsylvania's Wharton Business School, "The Donald" spent his next five years in his father's real estate business, which was valued at that time (in the 1980s) between $100 million and $500 million.

Where this archetype fails us is that we read books by Trump and attend his seminars where he is supposed to teach us how we can get rich "just like him." Unfortunately, we can't use the same method because he started with the wealthy resources that 97 percent of the people in the United States[8] do not have, namely, millions of dollars from his father. We mistake Trump's story as archetype one, something from nothing, when it is really an example of archetype two where the rich get richer.

In a recent issue of a pop-culture magazine, one of the headlines read, "'How to Get Rich,' by Ivanka Trump."[9] I did not even have to read the article to know the answer—have "The Donald" as your father! Many rich-get-richer stories are disguised as something-from-nothing stories to deepen the dramatic effect.

Unless we are rich, most of us don't much appreciate the advantages that rich people have in making even more money, but, like it or not, wealth brings definite advantages. Rich people don't pay interest; they collect it. Rich people don't pay rent; they invest in property. Rich people don't blindly pay taxes; they hire someone to manage their taxes down.

There is no question about it. The easiest way to make money in business is to start with a lot of money, and there's absolutely nothing wrong with that. It's actually very logical, but let's not be confused. The stories of archetypal achievers like Donald Trump (and now Donald Jr., Ivanka, Eric, and presumably baby Baron when he gets old enough) are not rags-to-riches or something-from-nothing stories, but rich-to-richer tales.

The second place this archetype fails us is that just because you start out rich or become rich does not mean that future financial success is guaranteed to you. Trump is also a compelling example of making *and losing* a lot of money over the course of his career.

Archetype Three: The Comeback—*Rocky* Revisited

The third archetypal road to success is perhaps even more an American pop-culture favorite than the something-from-nothing myth. It is supported by the overused motivational phrase, "If at first you don't succeed, try, try again." This scenario features failure as a stepping-stone to success (as represented in Figure 2.3).

It goes like this: Start with a series of miserable failures; get down to your last dollar (it adds to the drama if you are on some type of public assistance); and then, just when all seems completely lost, an unlikely event or product delivers an amazing, unexpected, and usually unintended financial result.

It even seems that this recovery from failure is guaranteed somehow in the grand plan—as if the failures were trials to make you *earn* your success. In this ilk, the original failures of popular cultural idols such as Elvis Presley, Marilyn Monroe, John Kennedy, the Beatles, and Madonna are well known.[10]

Like many other people, my favorite failure-to-success story is that of Harry S. Truman, whose clothing store went bankrupt after World War I. As our country's 33rd president, he was still sending checks to his creditors—and presumably they were still cashing them.

A more current example is Paul Orfalea, who, as a dyslexic second-grader, was put into a school for the mentally retarded for six weeks. In 1970, Orfalea founded Kinko's, the most successful photocopy center in America, which he sold in 2004 to Federal Express for $2.4 billion.

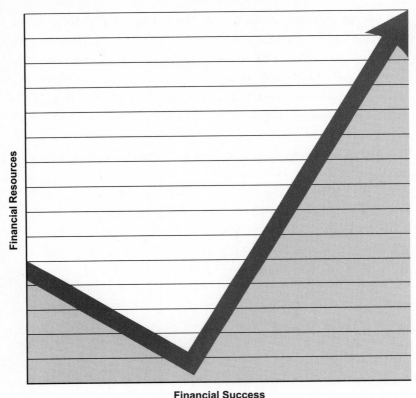

FIGURE 2.3   Archetype Three: The Comeback

John Grisham's first novel, *A Time to Kill,* was reportedly rejected by 16 agents and many publishing houses. In 1989, Wynwood Press finally published 5,000 copies of the book, many of which never sold. Grisham went on to become the best selling author of *The Firm, The Pelican Brief,* and dozens of other novels. He ranks among the best-selling authors of in the 1990s.[11] Eventually, *A Time to Kill* sold millions of copies and was made into a movie in 1996.

Simon Cowell, the famous judge on the hit reality show *American Idol,* experienced a lot of failure before hitting it big. His record label, Fanfare Records, went out of business in 1989, and he owed the bank over $1 million.[12] He lost everything and had to move back in with his parents. Cowell reinvented himself on *Pop Stars,* a show that originated in Australia and was brought over to England. After *Pop Stars,* Cowell and Simon Fuller (owner of 19 Entertainment) conceived of a show called *Pop Idol,* which followed the now well-known formula: Audition, perform, and win by public vote. Cowell didn't take an ownership stake, but instead receives royalty rights for his label on every recording released by an *Idol* performer. Eventually Fox Network bought the show. *Pop Idol,* Simon Cowell, and *American Idol* have become huge hits. Cowell receives $8 million per season, the highest-paid Fox network star. In 2003, Cowell sold half of his S Records for $43 million to Bertelsmann Music Group.

Finally, my sons love to recount the story of J.K. Rowling, now the richest woman in England (and that includes the Queen).[13] Rowling reportedly started writing the story of Harry Potter in 1990 when she was caught on a delayed train between Manchester and London. She left England for a brief period to teach English in Portugal and continued to write about Harry. In 1993 Rowling returned to Britain and settled in Edinburgh. She was divorced with a baby. She struggled with depression. Unemployed and living on state welfare, she completed the first *Harry Potter* book by writing in local cafes whenever she could get her baby daughter to fall asleep. The rest, as they say, was magic.

All of these archetypal tales are familiar and fun to read. They bring smiles to our faces, warmth to our hearts, and stoke the will to financially succeed. However, we make a mistake if we rely on these examples as proof that if we "try, try again," we will succeed eventually. There are many more stories about people who tried and tried again, and never were able to succeed at their goal. We just don't hear about those.

Danger Ahead: Focusing on These Archetypal Outcomes Can Sting

In 2006, Chad Hurley, Steve Chen, and Jawed Karim of YouTube.com, who had started their company in a garage a little more than a year before, sold their business to Google for $1.65 billion. The business world immediately lauded this achievement as yet another example of how brilliant, young entrepreneurs can make over a billion dollars out of nothing in just 18 months. Sounds like archetype one, doesn't it?

People will now study YouTube's model and try to duplicate it. But the fact is that their success was an outcome at a particular point in time and is highly unlikely to be repeated—just as the road that eBay, Amazon, or Google took to success, if duplicated, is highly unlikely to yield similar fantastic results.

The second problem is that YouTube really is not an example of the something-from-nothing archetype. Chad Hurley was one of PayPal's first employees and the son-in-law of James Clark, the founder of Netscape and Silicon Graphics (do I smell archetype two here as well?). Venture capitalists were calling YouTube, offering funding within months of the start of their company. As brothers Chip and Dan Heath say in their *Fast Company* article about this, "That's not quite as uplifting as hearing that twenty-something buddies created a cool site to swap videos with friends."[14]

I recently talked to a young entrepreneur in New York City. He was trying to decide whether to move to Los Angeles to become an officer at a new start-up similar to YouTube, or stay in New York with his girlfriend to start their own company (which is what he really wanted to do). He had lost his passion for and belief in the Los Angeles firm, but he felt he had to join them because he thought that is what young entrepreneurs do and California is where they go.

He felt that if he followed this path, in three years he would be successful and wealthy like the founders of YouTube (archetypes one and two). His biggest concern was that if he did not join this company, someday he would read about their success in the newspaper and regret that he missed out on it. He likened this to how Pete Best may have felt when he was replaced as drummer of the Beatles at the last minute by Ringo Starr.

This is a compelling example of why these archetypal stories, while they are fun to retell, hurt the aspiring businessperson in the long run. We try in vain to follow a prescribed path to success which no one except the people who already achieved it can really follow. We also focus only on the published outcome, not the actual starting point or the process it took to get there. We fall into a trap that Mark Twain described for us long ago: "What gets us in trouble is not what we don't know. It's what we know for sure that just ain't so."[15] The archetypes are simply outcomes, not necessarily the makings of a successful process.

Copycats Need Not Apply

Why did best-selling author Dan Brown have to write so many books before he hit blockbuster status with *The DaVinci Code* (Doubleday, 2003)? He wrote a handful of financially unsuccessful novels until he wrote *The DaVinci Code* in 2003. What is so strange about this book (other than the fantastic assertions in the story) is that it is essentially the same novel as a book Brown had published a few years before, entitled *Angels and Demons* (Atria, 2000). Both books involved the same lead character, Robert Langdon. The plots are similar except that *The DaVinci Code* happens in France, and *Angels and Demons* is placed in Italy.

Was *Angels and Demons* just a bad title compared to *The DaVinci Code*? If *Angels and Demons* had been called *The Michelangelo Code* would Brown have had raging success two years earlier? *The DaVinci Code* was on the *New York Times* best seller list for 164 weeks (three years) and was subsequently made into a big production movie. *Angels and Demons* is now a best seller, too.

The message of these three archetypes is that when you work hard, have more money than anyone else, or keep trying regardless of setbacks and pain, you will succeed. However, there are plenty more stories of people who did pretty darn close to what the well-known examples of these archetypes did, yet failed—miserably, piercingly, and sometimes permanently.

This is why having true business confidence becomes so critical in developing a road map to your personal success. Without it, we lock onto one of these archetypes of success and try to ride someone else's dream and duplicate their path to riches.

But Wait—Doesn't Success Breed Success?

Usually these road-to-success archetypal stories conclude right after the person has made his fortune. This outcome satisfies most of us sufficiently, and we are not really interested in the rest of the story. But what happens to some of these successful people afterwards and over the long run?

Regardless of how they get there, once a person achieves financial success, is he *guaranteed* to stay at this plateau or climb even higher, as we are led to believe? Does success always breed more success? Unfortunately, the answer is no.

One of the reasons that we work so hard to achieve success is because we are taught that success is the only thing that builds and expands a businessperson's confidence, and that confidence will then bring more success. If this is true, then the corollary is that in order to have the courage to go on to even bigger business adventures, success is the required first step.

If you learn only one thing from this book, let it be that this supposition is pure nonsense No business journey is linear; a person can develop true business confidence whether they ever succeed or not.

Certainly, great financial success can breed confidence, but that kind of confidence often lacks balance and can quickly morph into less useful qualities like unbridled bravado, arrogance, and greed. This is being confidence crazy! Confidence run amuck can lead to eventual bankruptcy and in some cases jail time.[16] Newspapers are littered with stories of business executives who fell from more than financial grace.

And what about all the people who succeed wildly (seemingly following one of the three archetypes) and then have a series of failures and never recover financially or emotionally? What happened to the confidence that supposedly guaranteed their future success? Why didn't their resounding success breed more success? Was their first success merely luck? Did something block them from achieving more success? Did they not learn what they were supposed to learn from their failure, or how to apply the lesson? Did they think they had the Midas touch? And when they fell, did they fall too far down to come back?

Failure at the Very Top

Finding quantifiable research in this area is difficult since we rarely hear from failures again. These people seem to hide underground and just fade away from the reach of even an extensive Google search.

There are some examples of fabulously successful people whose post-fortune fate is well known. Consider the tragic story of Roy Raymond, who founded Victoria's Secret, a women's lingerie store originally based in California. Raymond, a graduate of Stanford University, became dissatisfied with working in large corporations. The idea for Victoria's Secret reportedly came to him while buying lingerie for his wife.

In 1977 Raymond started his own boutiques outside San Francisco with $80,000 (half of it borrowed from his parents). Five years later he sold the company to The Limited. After that, he experienced one business failure after another. Eventually, he lost the entire $4 million he had received for the lingerie company and declared bankruptcy. Eleven years later, at the age of 47, Raymond still owed a $77,000 tax bill.

On August 26, 1993, he parked his Toyota at the end of the Golden Gate Bridge, walked to the middle of the east sidewalk, and jumped, falling 220 feet to his death. I do not know why Raymond jumped or if factors besides his financial defeats contributed to his suicide, but it certainly seems that by not being able to recover from his many failures, Raymond saw no choice but to end his life.

A less terminal fate happened to one of this world's best inventors, Steve Wozniak, the college dropout who founded Apple Computers with Steven Jobs. The success and innovation of this company remains legendary. In 1981 a plane that Steve was flying crashed, and he had anterograde amnesia for five weeks, a common result of car crashes and other similar accidents in which one can't make new memories. After his release from the hospital he continued to work at Apple.

Then he left (or it may be more accurate to say he was invited to take a break from Apple) to finish his degree, and created a music festival called the U.S. Festival that cost him millions of dollars but didn't make a profit.

In 1985, Wozniak left Apple permanently. His next company, Cloud Nine, produced programmable remote controls for consumer electronic devices. It failed because the product didn't work well with some equipment and was not adopted by manufacturers. Reports at the time said this failure was so disheartening for Wozniak that he could not program software any longer.

"It gets to the point where you can't tell where the inventiveness was lost," he said not long after the Cloud Nine dream died.[17] Wozniak reportedly lost much of his Apple fortune. He then went back to school and became a teacher who held classes for elementary school kids in his own garage.

In March 2006, Wozniak shut down his latest company, Wheels of Zeus, which targeted the global positioning market. Being a teacher, of course, is an honorable job that can influence the future of many students, but why is it that Wozniak was unable to repeat his business success?

Was his success at Apple simply due to being in the right place at the right time? Was it his partnership with Steve Jobs that made him a financial superstar? Jobs also had failures after Apple, including Next Computers, the Newton, and Lisa while at Apple, but he was able to come back and reshape Apple and successfully create the hugely popular animation studio, Pixar.

Being an automotive hobbyist, one of my idols is Malcolm Bricklin, a legendary entrepreneur who "has made millions, but has also declared personal bankruptcy; he has attracted huge investors but has also been sued by his business partners."[18]

Bricklin achieved initial success in 1968 by establishing Subaru in America (under contract with Fuji in Japan), which made him $150 million.[19] He then failed with his gull-wing sports car (1971 Bricklin SV-1), which caused the province of New Brunswick to lose its investment of $23 million.[20] His importing of the Fiat Spider sports car and his inexpensive budget car the 1985 Yugo met similarly poor financial fates. He now wants to sell 100-mpg hybrid vehicles that would be priced less than gasoline-powered cars.

There are no predictable patterns in any of these situations of failure. Sometimes success leads to success. Sometimes failure leads to success, followed by failure, and then success again. Sometimes success leads to failure and never back to success. About the most we can say is that neither failure nor success is a prerequisite or a guarantee of more failure or more success.

The Roulette Wheel of Success

When you spin the roulette wheel in Las Vegas, regardless of whether red comes up 3 or 20 times in a row, the likelihood of the next spin being black isn't affected. The true odds are almost 50-50. (Those two pesky green spaces 0 and 00 keep things slightly tilted toward the house.) That's because after every spin, the wheel starts over. Nothing has changed (except you may have more or fewer chips). The wheel is still the same wheel. There are exactly the same number of red and black slots as there were before.

However, in life, every failure and each success changes something forever so that the path after each event is never predictable. There are just too many variables—and that can be perceived as good or bad, depending on where you are on the path.

Just as it is impossible to find a person who has never failed, it is equally difficult to find a person who has never succeeded at anything (although at some points in our lives all of us may have felt that way).

Many of us never reach an outcome that would even remotely be identified as the pot of gold at the end of the rainbow. If we are lucky enough or good enough to get there, it's usually not in quite the way that the archetypal models of success promised. And once we do arrive at success, there is no guarantee we will stay there; there is no guarantee that we will know how to use our financial success wisely, or that it will add to our happiness. This is where the cruel hoax lies. Ask anyone who has fallen off the beautiful, brightly colored rainbow to land lying face down in the rain. They are called one-hit wonders.

CHAPTER 3

I 've Got
Your One-Hit
Wonder:
867-5309

I have always been fascinated by one-hit wonders in popular music because they represent clear examples of people who were able to have a single financial success in a chosen career. Sometimes one-hit wonders go on to forge successes in other jobs or other areas of their life, but in popular music, they only made it once. By definition, if you are a one-hit wonder, you've failed.

Billboard magazine charts are littered with one-hit wonders—musicians who had just one Top 40 song and then never hit the charts again. These artists are generally only known for their one hit, and then their reputations quickly fade after that song falls off the charts. We might remember the song or be able to hum the tune, but we almost never remember the artists who sang it, unless we're some kind of trivia buff.

In 1996, Hollywood produced a movie about this phenomenon. *That Thing You Do!* is about a fictional 1960s band called The Wonders who broke up after one hit single.[1] By my count, the 1960s produced 400 one-hit wonders, and each subsequent decade has produced at least another 200.

Why is it that so many apparently successful musicians who sell a million copies of one song are never able to do it again? This one hit could have been the first song they ever wrote or the hundredth; it doesn't matter. Somehow, this song struck a chord in the public this one particular time. Not before and never after was the musician able to catch lightning in a bottle and get another composition onto the *Billboard* Top 40 list. It seems totally random and unpredictable. Should this phenomenon be characterized as abject failure or as a singular success?

In Chicago in the early 1990s, one of my neighbors was Michael Borch, drummer in the band The Ides of March, the rock group that had one Top 10 hit (number 2 on the *Billboard* charts) with "Vehicle" in 1970 and won a Grammy. "Vehicle" is a simple song about a guy attracting a girl with his car.

As Jim Peterik, the lead singer and songwriter of the group, describes it, the inspiration for the song came from Karen, a woman he met who broke up with him after six months dating. Some time later Karen called Jim and asked him to drive her to her modeling school in his beautiful 1964 Plymouth Valiant. He recounts how he felt like the king of the world riding next to her. This continued for a few weeks as he drove her different places. As Peterik tells it, the relationship remained very platonic, and out of frustration he told her, "You know, all I am to you is your vehicle." Thus the lyrics to "Vehicle" were born, and Karen is now Jim's wife.

These are not unusual lyrics. There is nothing unique about a teenage guy driving a fancy car to attract a girl. This is typical stuff to which many of us can relate. No one could look at these lyrics and predict that this would be a runaway hit. However, because of the popularity of "Vehicle," The Ides of March went on to play with rock legends like Led Zeppelin, Janis Joplin, and the Grateful Dead.

When I listen to "Vehicle" I can hear my neighbor Borch playing the drums in the background. He told me about playing at huge open-air concert stadiums in the 1970s and how electricity (and other things, too) filled the air. The next song from The Ides of March, "L.A. Goodbye," only made it to number 73 on the *Billboard* chart. While Peterik went on to have other hits in the band Survivor, Borch now sells security systems in Chicago. The Ides of March had that one hit, that one time.

Another well-known one-hit wonder is Tommy Heath. Most American music fans remember him as Tommy Tutone, although that is actually the name of his band rather than a person. Tom Heath's song "867-5309" ("the Jenny song") reached number 4 on *Billboard*'s Top 40 in 1982 and proceeded to drive phone companies across America absolutely crazy.

It's the type of song that when we hear it, we can't get it out of our head. Whether we're sitting in our office, car, or home, we're bound to hum the tune for hours, repeating that same phone number over and over again. We can't think of any other Tommy Tutone hits, because there aren't any. In spite of no new hits in more than 20 years, one thing is certain: Tommy Heath and his band, Tommy Tutone, made their permanent mark on pop music history. Heath continues to write and record, but he works as a software engineer to pay his bills. Is the band's work a success or a failure?

How does it feel to get just one hit? Lousy because we could not repeat it, or fantastic because at least we got across the finish line that one time?

Yvonne Brown was in the band New Colony Six in the 1960s when their two Top 40 hits made the charts: "I Will Always Think about You" (number 22 in March 1968) and "Things I'd Like to Say" (number 16 in December 1968). Before joining the New Colony Six, Brown had toured Chicago with another band. When that group broke up, she answered calls for auditions from the musical and drama section of the *Chicago Tribune* and got the New Colony Six job. Since the band was already on the MCA label, they were booked for a lot of great performances. She remembers performing at a large outdoor concert with the Beach Boys and Bachman Turner Overdrive. Brown recalls:

> Wherever we went, we would always have fans and they wanted to hear those two songs. As a speaker today, I integrate New Colony Six into my opening about who I am. There are still today people who come up to me and reminisce. It feels righteous because it's something you put your heart and soul in, and brought you so much joy. It was meaningful, and it still means something to others. It's great when you are not forgotten.

Yvonne Brown, who is now an author, speaker, and trainer, has no regrets about not having more hit songs with the band. She is satisfied that she got to a place that so many people never reach.

> If you have a hit at all, then you have something unique that not everybody in the world has. You were on stage, creating your art, and there were people in the audience who connected with that, and it created warm memories of their youth, and they come up and tell you about that. That one moment in time helps create who you are today.

Having that one hit gave Yvonne the confidence and bounce that she needed to succeed in her next career.

Following Yvonne's evaluation of the benefits of being a one-hit wonder, is there anything wrong with only hitting it once in business? Is our business life a failure if we only have one true financial success? Maybe once is all anyone needs. Mark Cuban, the owner of NBA basketball team the Dallas Mavericks, and former Internet billionaire (after selling Broadcast.com to Yahoo! in 1999 for $3 billion), has the answer to this question. He believes you only need to hit it once.[2] In one of his blog posts, he writes about relative success in sports.

> In baseball you have to get a hit 30 percent of the time. If you get an extra ten hits per hundred at bats . . . [you] make the Hall of Fame. In business, the odds are a little different. You don't have to break the Mendoza line (hitting .200). In fact, it doesn't matter how many times

you strike out. To be a success in business you only have to be right once. One single solitary time, and you are set for life. . . .

It doesn't matter how many times you fail. It doesn't matter how many times you almost get it right. No one is going to know or care about your failures, and neither should you. All that matters in business is that you get it right once. Then everyone can tell you how lucky you are.

For the financial success part of our goal, I agree with Cuban. It really does not matter how many times we fail, only that we succeed once. Bounce can take root with just one success. Wayne Gretzky pointed out that "You miss 100 percent of the shots you don't take."[3] We mustn't get caught up in the failures. It only matters that we met our success requirements that one time. When things go bad, we can think back to that one time where perhaps the planets aligned, and we got to the goal line.

My uncle, Fred Carman, who is over 80 years old now, still talks of how he was a football player in school. He likes to recount the day that he intercepted four passes and returned two for touchdowns in one game. He is still listed as number three on the all-time longest punt returns in U.S. high school history.

So instead of focusing on the times where the prize got away, it's perfectly fine if, like those hundreds of one-hit wonders and my uncle Fred, we can focus on the times that it went perfectly as planned or that we achieved the result we wanted, no matter how the execution went.

With true business confidence, we can look back at a single success and enjoy it for what it was. Maybe there *is* only one success on a particular path. We may need to bounce to an entirely different path to achieve another success. The complete answer to this puzzle can't be known until the end of our lives.

The order of successes and failures does not diminish the high point. Hitting it once can help root a sense of business confidence that will carry through whether the rest of the path is filled with failure, success, or a mix of both. In fact, for people who have the one big score toward the front end of the life game, the resiliency spring becomes even more important because they will be needing it for the rest of their life.

No one actually remembers our failures more than we do. But fighting with failure demons does give us an important skill that will ultimately boost our ability to bounce. Forget the outcomes. Forget about bouncing back to any particular place. Just bounce!

CHAPTER 4

The World from Here: Start Where You Are

B usiness is conducted differently in different countries around the world, with diverse sets of challenges and expectations. This is an eye-opening fact for some Americans who believe the entire world speaks English and does business in U.S. currency.

There is also a widespread belief in the rest of the world that American businesspeople have it easy when it comes to success and failure. This difference was highlighted by Alexis de Tocqueville, the French aristocrat whose observations of American character constitute one of the most influential pieces of literature from the nineteenth century, *Democracy in America*. In the 1830s de Tocqueville and Gustave de Beaumont were given an 18-month leave to study the penal system in the United States. When they arrived, they were surprised to learn that this country did not have debtor prisons as in England, where if you did not pay all your bills you went to jail.

To this day, other cultures perceive that in America, businesspeople (at least owners and entrepreneurs if not their employees) are allowed to fail, recover from this failure, and get at least one second chance and often more to rebound. Colin Jones, a professor at the University of

Tasmania in Australia, observes that, "I sense in America that failing is part of the educational process of becoming an entrepreneur."

This perspective is significant because now, more than ever before, we are all part of a global economy. That means that American companies, large and small, are doing business in other countries—not just sales but operations—and that more immigrants than ever before are entrepreneurs in the United States. The beliefs and realities of all these cultures are coming together in new and often expected ways.

The "Failure Is Not an Option" Cultures

For almost 10 years, Andria Lieu has run a fashion clothing business in Chicago. She was born in Vietnam and is the youngest of five children. When Andria was 12, she and her family were forced to flee their homeland during the North Vietnamese takeover. They arrived at a refugee camp on an island in Malaysia where they awaited sponsorship to immigrate to a new home. Andria's family received an invitation from a small town in Michigan, which is where Andria lived before she came to Chicago.

While she has grown a very financially successful business, Andria still views *any* failure as a personal deficiency. She believes that "failure means that I'm not strong enough, that I'm weak, and that I'm not smart enough." She sees failure as a character flaw. It comes from the inside out, not from the outside in. According to Andria's view, failure is something that is totally our responsibility and within our control. If we fail, it is solely a result of something we did or did not do. External factors have little or no influence.

As you might imagine, these beliefs place a tremendous amount of pressure on Andria to succeed. In this sense, *she is* her success or her failure. This imparts a huge sense of personal responsibility and dedication that often produce great results; unfortunately, there is no separating yourself from your business. In Andria's world, if you fail, you are trapped forever in a personal purgatory. In such "failure is not an option" cultures, there is a constant pressure to produce. Being successful, however, does not create true resiliency or anything like bounce, because there is remains the ever-present, fearful opportunity of failing.

Andria's attitude is reflected in many Asian countries where, if you financially fail at business, you are literally forced to move out of your city, region, or country because the stigma of failure is so large. A student in a class that I was addressing at Thunderbird University in 2005 described how her parents left Taiwan after her father had failed. In order to have any future, she explained, they had to leave. While the increased physical mobility in this century allows people to start over in another place far from their home community or country, it doesn't erase these deep-seated internal cultural attitudes or the opinions of family and friends.

A. A. Gill, British newspaper columnist and writer, reflects about how Japanese culture affects the way that business is done:

> A Japanese man tells me that the key to understanding Japan is to grasp that it is a shame-based culture. In the West success is the carrot. In Japan, fear of failure and ostracism is the stick. This isn't merely a semantic difference, it's a basic mindset. Westerners trying to do business here complain that it is impossible to get decisions made. The Japanese negotiate for months without saying yes or no. Nobody wants to lay his face on the line; there is no comeback from failure. Decisions emerge out of group inertia. Japan manages to be both rigidly hierarchical and enigmatically lateral."[1]

Nick Papadopoulos grew up in a traditional Greek family; his is the first generation to work in America. To him, success and failure are solely a matter of effort. "From the traditional Greek perspective, failure is not working hard. Failure is not doing what it takes, not being resourceful. Failure is making excuses."

As a professional sales coach, he feels, like Andria, that success and failure are totally within a person's control. If only you work hard enough and long enough, you can succeed at anything. This again leads to a great work ethic—and back to archetype number three.

In Australia and New Zealand, the business environment can also be very difficult, but in a different way. People there practice their own particular version of *schadenfreude*, which means to experience satisfaction at another's failure.[2]

Colin Jones told me when I visited his college in 2005 that "in Australia, people want to see you fail. Everyone wants to say, I told you so; I told you it was never going to work. You have to find a way to insulate yourself from all the negativity. We have a thing, 'Tall Poppy Syndrome,' which simply means that people will always be trying to bring down the high achievers." (When farmers grow poppies, they typically cut off the tops of those that are growing too fast, in an attempt to maintain homogeneity.)

Studies have shown that in Australia and New Zealand, people are averse to risk. Australians fear failure, and this has an impact on their desire to start new businesses. Although achievement is privately respected, a failed business is a huge defeat that many entrepreneurs are just not willing to risk.[3]

One person interviewed in this study went further and said that "while one is encouraged to learn from it, so that mistakes can be avoided next time, I don't believe people can be *proud* of failure in Australia and would naturally wish to hide past mistakes if they are wanting to secure investment, support, or employees for their next venture, or even if they were simply completing a regular job application." As a culture, they are very quiet about failure and even overlook it a bit because they see it as so embarrassing.

New Zealanders and Australians actually admire what they think is Americans' willingness to fail. But they see failure as a stigma, not a badge of honor. This contributes to the lack of serial entrepreneurs in those countries. Most people interviewed felt, after they had risked it all once, why tempt fate and do it again? Other New Zealanders feel that they lack the passion to keep expanding their business, especially after some initial success.

"We despise the growth mania that we hear Americans talk about, the compulsion to get more customers," says Howard Frederick, who tracks the country's small businesses at Unitec New Zealand, an Auckland university. "Here it's 'More customers? That's a bother.'"[4]

Johan Wiklund, a professor at the Jönköping International Business School in Sweden, studied whether Europeans would or would not do business with people who have failed before. In the United States, 45 percent of the people surveyed would not do business with people who had failed. In Sweden, almost 70 percent would not do business with someone who had failed. That refusal percentage was also significantly higher in Denmark and Finland, and 10 percent lower in Austria, Germany, France, and Spain.

Wiklund believed that severe punishment for entrepreneurial failure reduced people's willingness to try. He stated that there are large potential losses compared to other career alternatives, so "Why bet the farm if you do not have to?" In Sweden, he said, severe punishment for entrepreneurial failure (lifelong payback of any debts incurred) brings too much chronic grief and economic burden for most people. There is no reason for Swedes not to play it safe.[5]

What a GEM!

The annual Global Entrepreneurship Monitor study (GEM) is a cross-national assessment of entrepreneurial activity in 35 countries. The study defines countries as having a high *failure index* when people are afraid to fail because of the ensuing social stigma or governmental penalties (e.g., prison time, lifetime payment).

The GEM study shows that a high index leads to a low rate of entrepreneurship except in high-necessity countries where they have no alternative (called *necessity-driven entrepreneurship*). In countries with a low gross domestic product (GDP), commonly referred to as the Third World, the economic necessity of the culture overrides the fear of failure. According to Gaston Arevalo of Venezuela, the majority of entrepreneurs there are motivated by necessity. "Since most people don't have access to the job market, they have no other option but to be self-employed."[6] In these cultures, if I want to feed my family, I simply need to deal with whatever risk I must take. These are *necessity cultures,* where the decisions become a lot simpler. They are working to fulfill the lower levels of Maslow's hierarchy of needs, where biological needs for food and shelter trump any desire for business self-actualization and self-esteem.

The GEM study suggests that there may be a relationship between the motivation to start a business and the chance of it actually succeeding. "For example, in countries with relatively low income and low levels of social security, high ratios of necessity are observed. In these countries, given the lack of viable alternatives, people may be starting businesses even though the prospects of their ventures may not be very favorable. In contrast, people in countries with high income levels and strong social security systems are not as likely to start a business with bad prospects."[7]

Laws Affecting Business Reflect Cultural DNA

Certainly, it is true that business failure is financially tolerated by the fairly liberal United States bankruptcy rules and laws. Until very recently in America, a businessperson could file for bankruptcy, have all his debts erased, and get credit again in seven years. Even though bankruptcy laws were tightened in 2005, the repayment environment remains considerably more liberal in the United States than in many other parts of the world.

In America, a failed businessperson can start over and get some help at the expense of his creditors. In other places in the world, it is not so easy. The more severe laws in other countries are supported by certain cultures' draconian and harsh view of failure.

Collin Anderson, the founder of Digital Innovation in Chicago, recounts a presentation by a person who works in the area of bankruptcy all over the world. He talked about how in the United States, bankruptcy is about the money. In Europe, it's about revenge. "They want to punish the guy who lost money. I do not know if this is true but I have heard in Germany, if you've lost money for investors, you are barred legally from raising money again."

In Chile, it is easy to lose it all the first time. There is a law "inspired by the market economy as an instrument to reassign productive resources and permit the transfer of the assets of a failed debtor for reintegration into the economy."[8] This suggests that failed debtors lose things quickly and severely. Their remaining resources are given to someone else who has not failed before.

China passed a new bankruptcy law in August 2006 that covers both state and private firms. "This new legislation will give creditors greater protection if a firm is bankrupt, whereas in the past redundant workers were paid off first."[9] The law for the first time allows businesses to have protection and reorganize instead of just going out of business. Protective laws similar to this one allow the business to fail and still have an opportunity to succeed again after an orderly reorganization.

According to the World Bank, on average, in the United States it takes only 1.5 years to resolve a bankruptcy at a cost of only 7 percent of the assets of the company. On average, 77 percent of the debts of the company are recovered. This compares favorably to much of Europe and Central Asia, where recovering from bankruptcy averages 3.5 years at a cost of 14 percent, with businesses recovering only 30 percent of the debts. In East Asia and the Pacific, it can cost 23 percent of the assets with a 27 percent recovery of the debts. In many African countries, it can cost up to 75 percent of the company assets and none of the debts get repaid.[10]

Where it is difficult to recover losses when a company fails or it costs a lot to recover debts, the society is a lot less forgiving of failure.

These laws and cultures make the penalty for business failure high; therefore people are less willing to risk failure and less likely to come back from it because the price, financially and socially, is so high.

Severe bankruptcy laws may also be a deterrent for a business to exit the market even when the owners or stockholders can see future failure written on the wall. Such severe laws can force businesspeople to keep going, burning more capital, and growing their debts to postpone the inevitable, such that when they ultimately have no choice but to go out of business, their losses are significantly greater and more damaging than if they had taken the step earlier.

In America, even if you fail miserably, you can still financially get another chance. With less reason for retribution, the stigma of failure is still there, but financially it does not follow you the rest of your life through an extended payment schedule or an ostracized relationship with your family.

The first building band is your *environmental and cultural DNA*. Your country's and culture's attitudes toward success and failure have a large impact on your ability to develop business confidence. Culture shapes the individual businessperson's tolerance and definitions of failure. In the United States, where the culture at least pays lip service to the idea that someone who fails can get another chance, businesspeople who do fail are not viewed as cultural pariahs as long as the failure isn't permanent. In fact, when they later succeed, they are viewed all the more positively *because* they had failed before. The believers in the archetypes of success welcome them home as heroes.

When people never succeed, they simply melt away, never to be heard from in the business context again. In countries where it is one chance and you are out, it becomes much more difficult to accept the risk since you will have only the one chance at achieving your financial goal.

The single biggest influence on culture in the United States is the fact that it is a society of immigrants. Millions of people come to the United States every decade from different cultures, looking to make a living or create a whole new life for themselves and their families. Many of them are escaping home countries where they felt unable to succeed or where they had failed miserably—some so miserably that they came here from foreign jails.

On the one hand, these first-generation American entrepreneurs don't have much to lose. They've taken some of the greatest risks a person can take—leaving home, family, roots, and going to a new place (sometimes even illegally) where they don't know the language and don't have a job. Likely they can't allow themselves the luxury of dwelling on fears of failure, and yet they must reconcile their cultural attitude toward failure with how they expect things to be (and how they really happen) in the United States. On the other hand, given the diversity of the U.S. business environment and the global economy, these country and cultural attitudes toward failure may create opposing forces in the individual's attitude and orientation.

Everyone starts from his own cultural bias and archetypal models. Whether popular culture has a permissive or dismissive attitude toward failure will influence the decisions you make and how you will respond when you fail. Zen Buddhists say that you need to "start from where you are." Listen to the voices of your own culture or environment. It is the first building band for true business confidence.

CHAPTER 5

Forget the Archetypes: Messy Lines Teach Humility

left IBM as a rising star in 1990, only to get fired from my new job after just 12 months. I was 31, newly married, jobless, and broke. Under these circumstances, humility comes pretty quickly. I felt horrible and guilty of failure. I could barely face all those around me who had so many high expectations of my promising career.

As one of my mentors described it, I was having a "crisis in confidence." My father commented that maybe IBM would take me back to my old job. A few years before, I had left IBM triumphantly, and now my father wanted me to crawl back. Feelings of shame and defeat raced through my mind.

I found two new business partners in the classified section of the *Chicago Tribune* newspaper. I realized years later that while it may be acceptable to buy a car or rent an apartment from an ad in the newspaper, that is not a good way to find a business partner.

Once again, I was kicked out of the business, this time by these partners. I was now 32, still a relative newlywed, the father of a newborn son, and really, *really* broke. What did I do next? A month later I started my third business, this time with a well-known business friend.

Things went along reasonably well for about three years, and then in May 1995, I woke up with blurry vision several days in a row. I went to see my doctor. Later that day, he delivered the news that I had a chronic disease that would probably cut my life short by 15 years. I remember sitting in the hospital emergency room, unable to make myself leave, reading the chapter from a medical textbook on all the bad things that could happen to me because I now had diabetes. Talk about a crisis in confidence!

I had learned to coexist with my disease, when five years later, I had another visit from fate. I lost my largest client, which forced me to lay off many employees. A few years after that, my best manager left, creating a vacuum of leadership that resulted in huge financial losses.

Were there successes in between these failures? Sometimes yes, sometimes no. In 1999, I sold my business during the Internet bubble. We all call that success. But whether mine is a "try, try again" success story or a string of one-hit wonders, we won't know until I quit or die.

In the interim, I decided to use my chain of failures to bring into sharp focus the fact that I, a reasonably astute and successful, hard-working business guy, have failed—over and over again.

Have Humility or Have It Bestowed upon You

No matter what we might have heard or even been taught in business school or anywhere else, humility is not a dirty word. To develop true business confidence, humility is a very desirable and necessary quality.

There are a lot of misconceptions about humility. Most of us become familiar with the term through the idiom "to eat humble pie"[1] when we need to apologize for an error. But true humility isn't groveling or being fearful, shy, or retiring. It doesn't mean always putting the other guy ahead of you. Humility isn't something you decide you want and then you develop it overnight. Humility requires experience, openness, and a willingness to take chances and to make mistakes—and sometimes even to look publicly dull.

As real businesspeople experience a veritable roller coaster ride of failures, bankruptcies, and breakdowns, they begin to discover the profoundly curvy and unpredictable lines of all these business lives. Those messy lines help create humility.

My Mother's Model of Success

I was not trained to ride the roller coaster when I was growing up. I loved my parents for telling me how wonderful my life would be. My mother painted the idyllic picture that every year I would get promoted, and every year I would accumulate more money. The way I heard it, my business life would look something like the path delineated in Figure 5.1.

And for a while, this is exactly what happened. At IBM, I was promoted and made more money every year. When I left IBM in the early 1990s to work with one of my clients, I still thought I was on the curve of my mother's model of success, and I confidently used its trajectory to calculate my future earnings on the backs of napkins and legal pads.

After all, I had been promoted every year that I was at IBM and had received consistent raises. Little did I know that my personal roller coaster was about to leave the station. I didn't hear those wheels grinding and straining as the lead car chugged up the hill. I was so busy looking up at the bright blue sky that when the car took that first swooping fall, I was stunned. As my experience and tenure grew in business, the land mines that I encountered made my career chart look like the one in Figure 5.2.

If this graph looks like your life, welcome to the well-worn path that most of us are on. And if you still think your path has been a linear line straight to the sky, you may either be kidding yourself, be full of ego-driven confidence, or else be at such an early stage in your

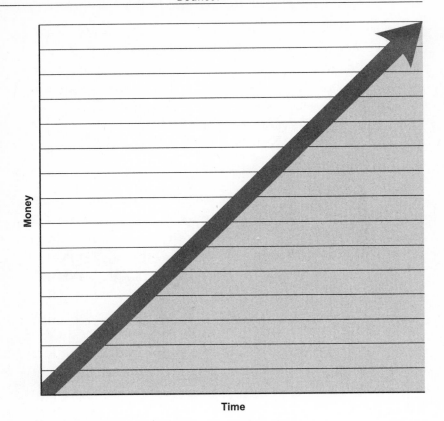

FIGURE 5.1 My Mother's Model of Success

career that you haven't yet had enough time in the trenches to create much of a time line or graph.

I did not start out as a humble guy. I was confident, ego-driven, and bold. As time went on, it was encountering failures (some of them dead-end with no specific lessons to teach) that helped my humility and eventually my true business confidence grow.

Don't despair because career lines are not linear. Messy lines create humility. Humility keeps us open-minded and allows us to learn. Humility makes it okay to fail and adds to our ability to bounce because we aren't struck down by our failures. As I think

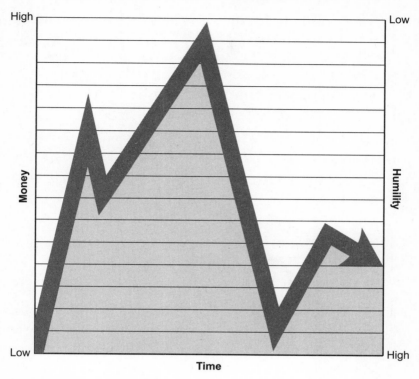

FIGURE 5.2 My Real Path

back now, perhaps my mother was setting me up to be overconfident so that I could learn humility when failure hit me in the face.

John Follis, who is the president of his own advertising agency, Follis LLC in New York City, was fired four times before he went on to start two successful businesses. He believes that he *needed* to be fired four times before he was able to meet and recognize a suitable partner to start a new agency.

After those four firings, Follis did find a partner and together they founded a new agency. But all was not well. Follis states that while he and his partner were winning awards for their projects and were even invited to the White House, something else was happening.

Inside it became painfully clear in the first six months that our partnership wasn't going to last. I kind of had that feeling in the beginning. It was a roller coaster that I was strapped into before I was even sure I wanted to do the ride. Four years later, I had shingles, back problems, and a radically constricted colon. Leaving that business was the easiest and the hardest decision I ever had to make in my life.

It takes a lot of humility to admit that what looked so right and ought to be so right has turned out wrong. In Follis's case, his sense of humility eventually overcame his ego, and he made the business changes that were right for him.

Cycle the Random Walk

What does it mean to possess and demonstrate humility in business?

The dictionary defines *humility* as "the quality or condition of being humble; modest opinion or estimate of one's own importance, rank."[2] Said another way, humility in business means that you realize you are vulnerable to the cycles of success and failure just like everyone else—that you are not in total control of your own destiny.

Business is random. No matter how good you are, how well you plan, how many degrees you've earned, or how much money sits in your bank account, someday, in some way, you are not going to succeed. That means that sooner or later, you, like all the rest of us, are going to fail. The other important thing to remember is that sometimes—no matter what a screwup you are—you will also succeed.

Humility means admitting that maybe you don't have the Midas touch (which, as the king's story attests, can sometimes turn out to be a very good thing). It also means that despite what our mothers told us, success is guaranteed to no one, no matter how smart, hardworking, educated, good looking, well positioned, or lucky a person might be.

This characteristic of business is similar to the 1973 "random walk" investment theory, created by Burton Malkiel. In his book

A Random Walk Down Wall Street (W. W. Norton, 2007, ninth ed.), he states that "past movement or direction of the price of a stock or overall market cannot be used to predict its future movement. Originally examined by Maurice Kendall in 1953, the theory states that stock price fluctuations are independent of each other and have the same probability distribution."[3] Random walk proposes that stock prices take an unpredictable path. "The chance of a stock's future price going up is the same as it going down. A follower of random walk believes it is impossible to outperform the market without assuming additional risk."

I have always found it interesting when sports players who have been performing well all of sudden hits a bad streak. They may regain their momentum and get back later in the year to another hot streak. Alternatively, they may be traded to another team as a result of this failing performance. Once on the other team, in a different situation, surrounded by different circumstances, they often thrive and become successful again. This doesn't always happen, but it does occur a surprising number of times.

Why? Does the additional-risk part of the random walk theory apply? Or are struggling players able to leave the baggage and the reminders of their failure behind? Are the expectations of the new team different? Is this what allows them to succeed?

These are all contributing factors. What this scenario suggests is that when we get to a new place or a new decision point, we have a fresh opportunity to succeed or fail if we are not burdened by the baggage of the past. We flip the coin one more time. It has the same chance of coming up heads or tails regardless of how it came up last time. Remember that success and failure are not straight lines.

Jeffrey Rosenthal, in his book *Struck by Lightning,* writes that we "love the thrill of a surprise party, the unpredictability of a budding romance, the mystery of a good detective novel, and the freedom of not knowing what tomorrow may bring . . . on the other hand, we hate uncertainty's dark side. From cancer to SARS, diseases strike with no apparent pattern . . . terrorists attack, airplanes crash, bridges collapse and we never know who will die next".[4] Rosenthal sees randomness as neither good or bad—it just *is*.

Linda Regulbuto, a former dancer, now works at the Bushnell Center for the Performing Arts. She loves not knowing what comes next. She compares the randomness of business to putting on a dance show. "You have no idea how much a show is going to make. You are living on the edge of the stage. One foot forward, you fall into the pit. One step back and you're in the limelight."

Randomness is hard for many businesspeople to accept and drives many of us crazy. We want to be able to control results. We want to figure out all the angles and contingencies and guarantee success. We think that if only we can do this, we will find a way never to fail.

Skate the Random Walk

There are ways to circumvent the random walk. You can guarantee (temporary) success in the stock market by trading on inside information. In spite of the risks and safeguards, many businesspeople still believe they are entitled to any advantage they can grab. But according to the law, this is not only cheating; it is illegal.

Do people resort to cheating and breaking the law because they buckle under to the seemingly unbearable pressure of trying to closely follow one of the success archetypes? Or do they simply run out of patience? Do they reason that the end (their quest for financial wealth) justifies the means?

People tend to look for the shortcut. We seek to somehow outwit fate or any other obstacle that gets in our way, and tip the scales in our favor. This is a further suggestion that our American culture only pays lip service to accepting failure as a part of success. If it were truly acceptable to fail in our culture, would so many businesspeople feel such a pull to resort to the many illegal and unethical tactics that they use to succeed or to give the appearance of success? Or is this a pattern produced by the craziness that takes over when humility is absent, making us feel entitled, deserving, or justified in doing whatever it takes to achieve one of the archetypal models of success?

This phenomenon is further complicated because, unfortunately, cheaters do not always get caught. In fact, in some cases crime pays very well. Bad guys win a lot. We all know this. But after years of looking at the equation, for me, cheating is no way to conduct business. It is not a comfortable way to live or the way I choose to make my contribution to the business world. I do stray infrequently, and in my business career I have used some tactics that I am not proud of—if you read my previous book you will hear about those examples. But at the end of the day, I want my success to come honestly, and I'm willing to bet that most other people do, too.[5]

To give you a taste of my misadventures, I bought new office furniture for a key client visit and then returned it to the store after the client left. I hired friends to work in my office for a day so that when a client visited, we appeared larger and busier than we actually were. I also constructed empty boxes to line our warehouse shelves so that clients would think we had more inventory and orders than we did.

The results of those actions didn't lead to real satisfaction no matter how much financial success we achieved. Fortunately, my mentors have always been there to bring me back to a more righteous place.

When I say in my lectures that there are no five repeatable steps to success, my audiences get jumpy, but there is simply no legal way to outthink or outflank every single business situation to absolutely guarantee success. At a recent conference at Harvard University, one student even shouted out, "My parents are paying a lot of money for an education here—you better give me the five steps for success or I won't be able to go home!" This is the "mother's model of success" again, rearing its head in our ambitious college students as they seek a linear path to success.

A Call from Your Three Sisters

Gaining true business confidence requires accepting that a successful outcome does not mean that the next outcome also will be successful. Similarly, a failure does not foretell more failure. Accepting these uncomfortable but inevitable truths will lessen your frustration and enable you to focus your energies on the project at hand.

The only thing you can control is your *response* to a particular outcome and whether *you* characterize any particular outcome as a failure or a success. This is a much more productive approach to failure than most people's first reaction, which is often one of defiance, denial, or disbelief. We say to ourselves that we can't believe we failed or that it was not our fault.

Homer, the Greek poet, wrote in the *Iliad* that Odysseus had a different way of dealing with failure. At one point, he lashed himself to the mast and screamed into the storm. Standing and screaming straight into the wind does have its advantages, but today, we probably would swallow two triple espressos at Starbucks to help us resist the failure and gear up for the fight.

At first, resisting feels good. We are doing something proactive that feels like control. But after a while it is exhausting, and it does not accomplish much. I am not saying that we should not fight failure or fight back, but sometimes other responses are more productive.

One possibility is to acknowledge that you are not totally responsible for your success. Humility is the quality that allows you to do this. Once you accept that you aren't totally responsible for your successes, you can also accept that you alone are not totally responsible for your failures. With humility, you accept the randomness of the final outcome.

Having humility means that you grasp that business and life can turn on a dime. At any moment, your strong personal or professional balance sheet could be worth less, if not totally worthless. Shakespeare would have called it fate. Maybe it is fate, or maybe it was your team, or perhaps total strangers had something to do with it. Runs of success won't last forever; you will be surprised by something that you could not foresee.

To the ancient Greeks, fate was personified by three sisters, called the *Moirae*: Clotho, who from cosmic forces spun the thread that made up life; Lachesis, who measured how long the thread was to be for each person and then assigned each their destiny; and Atropos, who was the smallest in stature and yet the most powerful because she could cut the thread anytime she desired.

Dean Koontz, in his book *Mr. Murder,* writes that "The trick was to stay in the good graces of the first two sisters [Clotho and Lachesis] without drawing the attention of the third [Altropos]."[6] This is a difficult balance with which we all struggle.

Many of us in business have received a call from fate that has changed our lives. It may have come from a family member, a physician, the police, an employee, a vendor, or our largest customer. Somehow, when we hung up the phone, our life or business was different— sometimes better, often worse. Despite being raised on "mother's model of success," this happened to me many times in my life.

David Friedman of Tricon Resources describes how fate helped him develop humility in business after he bought a large company that was on the verge of bankruptcy.

> I had to deal with angry creditors; I had to bring in 50 container loads of merchandise from four ports of the country. But, the day I bought the company, my uncle had a heart attack. I had to jump in and do a lot of financial stuff and before the week was out my mother was diagnosed with leukemia. I told my workers, for that acquisition, you're on your own. I had to take care of my mom. I got back seven months later and my partner decided to bail so I had to negotiate a buyout. I had close to $3 million in debt that was personally secured. So I had to rebuild from there. I kept my house, but lost my wife. I've been wandering around trying to figure out what to do. . . . I had to get serious by leveraging my experience and become a financial adviser.

Humility also means not personally taking the entire blame for things that failed or fell apart. Maybe it was the sisters of fate, maybe it was your team, maybe it was your planning, or maybe, just maybe, plain bad luck. Develop enough humility to cut yourself some slack when things go horribly wrong. That means not taking yourself so seriously during the high highs so that you don't add to the pain of the low lows. Having humility also means giving away some of the glow when success shines on you.

Humility reminds us to respect the power of our competitors, our customers, and just how vastly complicated the business world can be. It is like sailing on the ocean, riding the waves high, but respecting the power of nature, knowing that a storm can brew up at any moment with the power to seriously set you off course or, worse, sink your boat.

More Bad Weather Ahead: Blame-Storming

Humility, however, isn't a hall pass for blame-storming—in other words, excusing yourself by pointing the finger at someone else. Don't fall prey to the culture of some organizations that I think would actually want to bring back the ancient Greek tradition of hubris—where, by custom, people would take deliberate and public actions to shame an individual to make themselves feel better.[7]

Rick Holdren of the Appraisal and Mentor Group used to spend a lot of time trying to seek revenge on people who he thought caused his failure; now he deals with that differently.

> Everybody has things that go bad and go wrong . . . things that have happened where people I thought were friends turned around and did nasty, unspeakable things to me. . . . When I was young, I would think up scenarios to get back at people, stay awake at night saying how can this happen to me, I must be attracting losers. Now, as I get older, I write it all down on a piece of paper, I look at it, and then I say I've got to let it go for my own sake. Let it go, and move on to something else.

Businesspeople who avoid responsibility for their own actions aren't much in evidence in Asian cultures. Professor Sang Hoon Nam at the University of Victoria compares the reaction of managers to failure in the United States and Korea, as well as in Japan. He cites many studies of "managers in the United States that may avoid responsibility for failure while claiming credit for any success." This is different from Asian cultures. "Japanese managers and politicians are likely to claim responsibility for failures and catastrophes. . . . Japanese adults were more likely to attribute failures to their own abilities."[8]

Professor Sang Hoon Nam studied managers in Korea and the United States and concluded that "Asians tend to assume stronger responsibility for failure than their counterparts in North America." He believes that one cultural dimension affecting this is the Korean emphasis on the group versus the American culture of individualism. He found that Korean managers were more willing to either "resign or make a formal apology." These managers seem to put the group ahead of their own ego. The humility comes from the meaning and the power of the team.

Is There a Formula for Humility?

Being a one-hit wonder will get you to humility if you are striving for another hit. Not being able to repeat the magic of your initial success paints a good picture for you. But in business, the traditional formula is

$$H = S \times A/(F \times P \times T)$$

Where
    H = HUMILITY
    S = SUCCESS
    A = AWE
    F = FAILURE
    P = SURPRISE
    T = TIME

You gain humility by having your success lessened by your failure. This is multiplied by how much of a surprise this failure was to you and by how long it lasts.

Humility is the second building band for developing true business confidence.

Having humility can either weigh us down or lift us up. It weighs us down if we wallow in the failure that can come along with it. If we think about all the things that went wrong and how we are garbage, the world can look pretty bleak. But humility can also help raise us up as we realize and respect the forces of business.

With humility, we can define, achieve, and measure our own greatness. Humility frees us from the burden of own expectations as well as the expectations of others. I'm reminded of this every morning as I test my blood. I no longer have the expectation that my blood sugar range will always be normal (80 to 120); I'm a diabetic, after all. I accept whatever number comes up and readjust my insulin to get the best result when I test it again in four hours.

Humility allows us to celebrate the success we have and to forgive any failures that we cause or that come our way. In the *Star Wars* epics, Luke is constantly reminded to "use the Force." In business, humility is that same force. We can use that force to gain business confidence.

We can get in touch with how humility feels from looking at something very beautiful or powerful. When I gazed at the *Mona Lisa,* the Grand Canyon, or the Sydney Opera House, I felt humble. When I visited a tribal school in Kenya or watched my sons being born, I felt humble. With balanced humility, our confidence gets to be the right size. Confidence too big turns egocentric. Confidence too small turns inside toward shame, always wanting to eat that humble pie back in the kitchen instead of sitting at the winners' table.

The Ego Is Dead—Or Is It?

The ego's rightful job is to protect. But we need to protect, and not *punish,* in a balanced and appropriate way. Ego can use the person's feelings of shame to justify a bigger role for itself than is fitting. Think of how often a person who lacks self-confidence becomes a bully to overcompensate.

Recent business events offer plenty of examples of how business leaders' egos have become too large and central to their businesses. In many cases this has forced the downfall of their companies.

It's easy to understand how successful companies are personified by their leaders—especially leaders who are passionate. The leader becomes the brand, and the public and the company's customers begin to connect the company head's authentic and true business confidence with the company's products.

When we hear of Microsoft, we think of Bill Gates more than we do of Paul Allen. Dell Computers is synonymous with its founder Michael Dell.[9] Jack Welch has become General Electric to most of us, even though he is retired.

So publicity and public opinion reinforce the already strong egos that these leaders had to have in order to build their businesses worldwide. As much as advertising strives to push us to identify with the logo, as consumers it is much easier to identify with a person than with an entire company. Every major sports team in the world selects one or two players to be the face of the team for that year. As humans, we assign a personal identity to everything we can. In many ways, Bill Gates may always be Microsoft, and Richard Branson may always be the Virgin Group of companies.

But leaders' unbridled passion, strong egos, and belief in the absolute rightness of what they are doing sometimes causes them to stay the course when maybe they should quit. They use their own egos to gain the controlling hand in managing disagreement among other people in their organizations who may also have large egos and seek to challenge their authority or have their own agenda.

On a smaller scale, ego also gives most small business owners excess confidence in many circumstances when they should not have any. Bo Peabody, author of *Lucky or Smart? Secrets to an Entrepreneurial Life,* notes that the ego gives people the courage to "act like famous international CEOs even when they know they are only playing a role. And the ego is the force that allows entrepreneurs to get comfortable with their powerlessness and learn to love the word *no* instead of panicking in the face of it."[10]

A business leader's ego can be a powerful tool. However, no ego, no matter how strong, is as effective a tool as true business confidence, which comes from an ego that is in balance with humility.

Can We Dress Up the Ego and Pretend?

When I was first starting out in business two decades ago, established companies often didn't want to do business with start-ups, so in the beginning of most of my businesses, we pretended to be bigger and more successful then we were.

Similarly, many people in the early years of their careers are just acting out the role that people expect them to play. They do not feel comfortable in their chosen career or job. This is pretty normal since many of us feel that we are just pretending or faking it in many parts of our lives. This is the root of the expression, "Fake it until you make it." Other people more politely call it, "Acting as if . . ."

I now believe in acting as if, but also trying to keep the misrepresentation to a minimum. Maybe this is just my personal way of making the ends justify the means. I have always believed in selling something to a client, *then* figuring out how to deliver it successfully and profitably. This has gotten me into trouble a few times, but in the long run, it does stretch the possibilities of what I can do to build a profitable customer base. This brand of confidence comes from years of watching other businesspeople build what they thought was the perfect product, only to have no one show up to buy it.

However, things can get out of hand. Enter King Midas again. Peabody adds that the ego can lead businesspeople to start believing their own press. Like Mark Twain, he believes this will keep the businessperson from knowing what they do not know.

> Ego is also the culprit when entrepreneurs cling to their role as founder rather than turning their companies over to more capable managers. And ego is to blame when entrepreneurs can't work with odd people who are clearly smarter than they are, or when they fail to remain calm and gracious in all business situations. Use your ego when it is called for, and check it at the door when you sense that it will get in the way. Unchecked egos are the most destructive force in business.[11]

Interestingly enough, Ego, the Living Universe, was a Marvel comic book character created in 1966 by Stan Lee and Jack Kirby as the enemy of Thor.

> Like all celestial bodies, Ego evolved from gas and dust to become a planet. For some inexplicable reason, however, this particular planet achieved sentience and the ability to move of its own volition. Like all living organisms, Ego needs to consume matter to survive, and began absorbing space vessels and even other worlds. Ego is exceptionally intelligent . . . it suffers from a God complex and can be emotional if thwarted.[12]

Does the Marvel comic book character Ego sound like anyone you know?

The role of a healthy ego, according to Sigmund Freud, is to mediate between the id's "primitive desires (hunger, lust, rage) and the super ego (morality, taboos)."[13] Unfortunately, this ego many times contributes to the downfall of a company because it makes us confidence crazy.

For example, a founder may hire managers less skilled than he is because he doesn't want anyone in the company to be better than him. He projects his self-worth into the company and does not want it challenged. In this way, as an A player, the founder hires B players.

The B managers hire C employees. And then the organization starts to crumble from the inside out.

Think about it mathematically, using Figure 5.3 as a guide. If A is 90 percent effective and B is 70 percent effective, and both are involved in decision making, the result will be 63 percent successful. This builds a very weak organization, and the ego-driven founder fails at exactly what he is trying to achieve: leverage. He is unable to gain the leverage of other people's skills since they are so weak. The founder remains all powerful, and the company remains unable to grow.

Lea Strickland, president of F.O.C.U.S. Resources, agrees that "to acknowledge that we don't know everything or don't have expertise in one particular area may be one of the most critical and difficult things we can do. A far too common error young businesses make is recruiting experienced experts and then not utilizing their talents and skills on or in the business. Many times (if not most) the cause of this

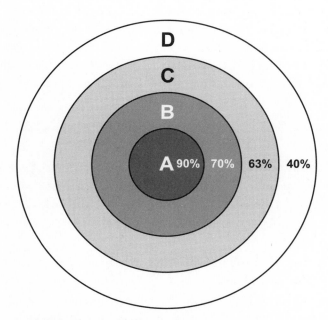

FIGURE 5.3   The ABCs of Hiring

error is ego or a fear of being undercut or displaced by someone with more knowledge or stronger skills."[14]

Our ability to get things done in a larger organization relies on hiring managers who are more skilled than we are or who plug the hole of one of our weaknesses. As business leaders, this is the only way to get the leverage we need to succeed. This is probably one of the most difficult transitions that a business founder needs to make.

When a company starts out, the organization looks like Figure 5.4—just one dot, the founder.

As the company grows, the organization becomes a series of dots all clustered around and reporting to the founder, as shown in Figure 5.5.

True leverage and growth in an organization happens when the founder is able to develop enough confidence to trust other managers in the company to grow the business, as represented in Figure 5.6.

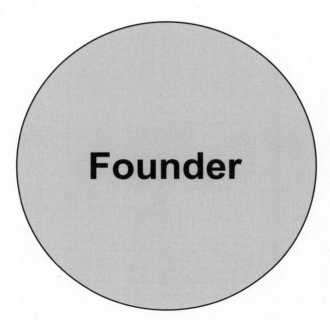

FIGURE 5.4   Chart of Original Organization

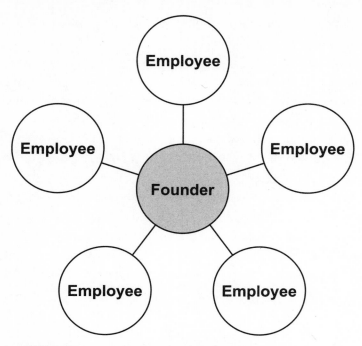

FIGURE 5.5   Key Organizational Elements

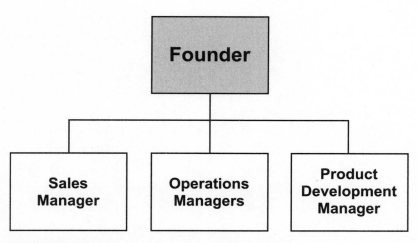

FIGURE 5.6   Chart of Hierarchical Organization

Peabody comes to the same conclusion regarding the potential negative effects of poor hiring on the workplace.

> I have often dreamed of a study that somehow measures the impact of ego on workplace productivity. In an ego-free company, all good ideas from all sources would be implemented. Managers would hire only people smarter than themselves, and would never spend valuable time worrying about who gets credit for what. Meetings would be shorter, as no one would feel the need to drone on in an effort to impress his colleagues and managers. In a business world devoid of egos, profits would rise, salaries would increase, and unemployment would plummet. In all seriousness: A number of the planet's problems would be solved.[15]

He describes a company driven by humility.

These Egos Have Left the Building without Humility

As fragile human beings, we need to take steps to control our egos. If we do not, incremental craziness starts to creep into our actions.

In recent years, we've watched as uncontrolled egos and the absence of humility brought down companies like Enron, WorldCom, and Tyco. Bernie Ebbers, the former CEO of WorldCom, was sentenced to 25 years in prison for allowing an $11 billion accounting fraud that destroyed his company. Ironically, Ebbers was quoted as saying, "You'll see people who in the early days . . . took their life savings and trusted this company with their money. And I have an awesome responsibility to those people to make sure that they're done right."[16] Of course, as we know now, he was doing just the opposite.

Dennis Kozlowski, Tyco's CEO, also received unauthorized compensation and sold $600 million of his company stock at record prices that were driven by fraudulent financial statements. In one of the most brazen examples in American history of ego gone awry, Kozlowski used Tyco funds to sponsor a $2 million toga birthday party on Sardinia for his wife. The results: Kozlowski and Mark Swartz, Tyco's CFO, were sentenced to up to 25 years in prison and ordered to repay

$134 million to Tyco. Kozlowski's wife divorced him soon after he was convicted.

After Enron became the United States' biggest corporate bankruptcy, corporate officers Kenneth Lay, former chairman, and Jeffrey Skilling, former CEO, were convicted of booking false profits to keep their stock price high. Enron's collapse cost 5,000 jobs and billions of dollars in shareholder value and employee pensions.

When the ego is in charge, it doesn't look for input. It makes its decisions based on what it thinks it knows—and ego-driven decisions are not usually the best ones for the business, the shareholders, the employees, or even the person making the ego-driven call, as Ebbers, Kozlowski, and Skilling have shown us with their actions.

After reading these accounts, we need to ask not whether a strong ego can live side by side with humility, but rather, is there any place in business for egos like these? Assuming that the answer is no, we next have to ask, what is the antidote to out-of-control egos like these? The answer is *humility*.

At one time or other, we've probably all heard the phrase "Check your ego at the door." This is more than just a platitude. With true humility, the ego does not have a job, can't run out of control, and won't cost us everything. The ego's role is to protect us. When you are following your own path with genuine humility and business confidence, there is nothing to protect.

Humility makes you able to see, hear, intuit, and interpret information that will lead to better decision making, which gives you the confidence to stay resilient. Absent the organic ability to produce this confidence, too often people in business fall back into being ego-driven and controlling; of course, the ego is only too happy to cooperate.

Humility Tells Us That We Are Not Our Businesses

Achieving a balance between humility and ego is difficult, not because of the driving conviction it takes to be in your own business, but because many entrepreneurs and small business owners are actually insecure. Failure hurts, and sometimes even when we achieve something, we continue to feel unworthy. This has a huge effect on anyone's business confidence.

According Larry Kanter at *Inc* magazine (September 2006), psychological research done in the 1980s estimated that two of every five successful businesspeople considered themselves to be frauds. Other studies have shown that upwards of 70 percent of people feel that way. Kanter comments that this is a strange combination since most of us think it takes much confidence to start and build companies. If you are a fraud, are you supremely confident or lacking it entirely?

Kanter notes that the situation is worse for women. According to the 2005 GEM Study, "women worldwide are less optimistic and less confident in their entrepreneurial skills and are more concerned about their failure."[17] This is exactly why it takes a particular type of confidence to be successful in business. It requires accepting the feeling that sometimes you feel like a complete fraud and other times you feel so completely confident in your task that people think you are crazy. Either way, you stay on the path.

Deborah House, CEO of the Adare Group, a financial consulting company, agrees. "First of all you need personal confidence—you have to know you're good at what you do. There's a fine line between gaining confidence and being arrogant and unwilling to accept that you don't know everything." Deep down, in order to develop bounce, you need to know that you are good at what you do. This does not necessarily mean every day, though.

Many of us work so many hours at business that it becomes very difficult to separate ourselves and our egos from our businesses, but to develop true business confidence, we must. Jim Blaha, a retired executive, is much more definitive and states that we need to separate our egos from our businesses: "I think it's a very important thing I learned long ago: When you're in business for yourself, you need to distinguish that your ego and your business are two very different things. If you understand that, your business can fail but then you will understand that *you* are not a failure."

Paul Bennett, CEO of Roomsof.com, literally had a crashing realization of this fact when in 2003, his cash resources became depleted in an effort to grow the company:

> Each day, it seemed that it took more Xanax to accomplish less and less. One day, I was driving on this highway and I was very, very groggy. The next thing I knew, I heard the loudest noise. I shot awake and I realized what the noise was: I was driving along the metal guardrail. It was like a can opener, slicing the right side of my car. I couldn't separate myself from my business. When it failed, I failed.[18]

According to Randall White, a principal at the Executive Development Corporation, it is especially difficult for men to separate themselves from their businesses. "It's the closest thing they have to the maternal feeling of having a child."[19] They are the company, both good and bad. Howard Book, an organizational consultant, puts it this way: "It's the third quarter was bad and there's something wrong with me."[20]

This separation between work, home, and self is becoming increasingly difficult with technology allowing us to blend all three too easily. Mobile phones and PDAs give us the ability to have the office wherever we are. Instead of shortening our workday, technology has lengthened it. If I didn't turn off my cell phone, PDA, and computer at 8:00 P.M., I could work all night.

Humility: Let's Talk about Mistakes

Have you ever met a pilot who wasn't confident? What kind of craziness is it that makes this group of people know with complete certainty (and be right) that tons and tons of metal can fly?

Most of us are reluctant to report it when we screw up; for pilots, it is different. When they make mistakes, the Federal Aviation Authority

(FAA) encourages them to report it.[21] The FAA even waives any penalties. The FAA gets it: In order for people to learn from mistakes, they have to be talked about. They want pilots to tell other pilots how the mistake was made.

Now part of the reason the FAA makes this so easy is that you can be fairly certain that no pilot ever wants to make a mistake. It's one of those professions where the people doing the work know with a very high degree of certainty that if they do make a serious mistake, they are likely to share the consequences—namely, to die from it. This reality removes the potential worry about intentional or careless mistakes, and makes it easy to assume that every rational pilot welcomes information and input that will prevent him from ever making a mistake the first time, much less making the same mistake that someone else already made.

Unfortunately, in the corporate world, the prevailing attitude regarding mistakes is about as far from the FAA's approach as you can get. We hide our mistakes for fear of being labeled a failure, feeling shame—or, worse, being subjected to retribution. Yet people do want to confess their mistakes, and we need to give them an environment to do it. We need to remember that when we do admit our mistakes, it can boost the company's credibility.

The Tylenol Drug Scare

In 1982, McNeil Consumer Products, a subsidiary of Johnson & Johnson, alerted the public that seven people in Chicago had died after taking Tylenol. The capsules turned out to contain cyanide. This created a nationwide panic. Johnson & Johnson (J&J) responded promptly by putting human safety first. The company warned consumers not to take any Tylenol products. (Imagine, a corporation telling you *not* to buy and use their products!) Subsequently, J&J recalled more than 31 million bottles of Tylenol valued at $100 million.[22]

Although no more cyanide was found in Tylenol, at the cost of millions more, the company offered to replace any Tylenol capsules consumers already owned with new tablets free of charge.

Johnson & Johnson demonstrated that it was a company led by executives who possessed an extreme degree of bounce. They were humble. They took ownership of any mistakes and full responsibility for their product. Initially, J&J's market value dropped $1 billion as a result of this incident, but five months later it had regained 70 percent of that.[23] It also made an entire industry better with safety caps. Today, J&J's market value is $180 billion.[24]

This was very different from what Source Perrier, acting from ego, did in a similar situation:

> An example of this was the crisis that hit Source Perrier when traces of benzene were found in their bottled water product. Instead of holding themselves accountable for the incident, Source Perrier claimed that the contamination resulted from an isolated incident. They then recalled only a limited number of Perrier bottles in North America. When benzene was found in Perrier bottled water in Europe, an embarrassed Source Perrier had to announce a worldwide recall. Apparently, consumers around the world had been drinking contaminated water for months. Source Perrier was harshly attacked by the media. They were criticized for having little integrity and for disregarding public safety.[25]

This incident of crazy confidence adversely affected Perrier for the next five years.

Humility Allows Us to Learn from Mistakes—Sometimes

Why do we repeat some mistakes over and over, while others we figure out the first time? Humility allows us to see our mistakes, learn from them, and not repeat them. Ego, by contrast, hides mistakes and, in a way, dooms us to repeat them until we screw up so badly our mistakes can't be hidden anymore.

I have always loved the expression, "Fool me once, shame on you; fool me twice, shame on me." Why *do* we consistently make the same mistake multiple times? Some of these mistkes are very big—and, one would think, very obvious.

We pick the wrong significant other. Many people marry and divorce multiple times (sometimes even with the same person). We go back to the same barber and get the same bad haircut. We return to a restaurant that serves bad food. We continue to do work for a client who owes us money. We consistently hire the wrong people for our companies. We trust someone who continually stabs us in the back.

Alternatively, there are other mistakes that we only make once. After I chose the wrong partners for my second business, I never made that mistake again (at least so far). The United States was unprepared for Hurricane Katrina and the levies breaking in New Orleans. It is unlikely (we hope) that the government will ever be quite that unprepared again.

We only stop repeating the same mistakes if the experience was so painful that we can feel the pain again when we approach the same or a similar situation. (Unless, of course, we enjoy the pain, but that would be a different book!) Learning to interpret our mistakes is really the key. Learn what there is to learn and then focus on the process instead of the outcome.

Humility Balances Ego

Humility leads to a balanced ego and an acceptance that many business results are beyond our control. Humility is not the absence of pride, but freedom from the burden of personal arrogance that tells us that we can and will, individually, determine our own futures.

A good example of this is Jing Ma, who is originally from China and now works as a senior auditor at one of the big U.S. accounting firms. In addition to her day job, she decided to help a start-up company, Jammin' Foods, get its products into various U.S. supermarkets.

After achieving initial success at Safeway, Jing Ma began concentrating on getting Jammin' Foods frozen food products into Giant. She understood Giant's purchasing patterns and knew it bought large quantities at heavily discounted prices.

Although this meant compromising Jammin' Foods' margins, Jing Ma believed that she could win the Giant account by placing her initial focus on establishing inventory turns and rapport. Jammin' Foods had limited production, so Jing Ma convinced the company to start holding inventory, which, of course, incurred additional cold storage costs. She tied up limited sales resources to track down people at Giant's purchasing department. She also covered the traveling expenses of brokers who had promising connections with the supermarket chain. In other words, she took a lot of risk.

Although she was very close to winning Giant as an account on several occasions, Jing Ma never was able to close the deal. She thought the ability to secure shelf space hinged only on her strategy, tactical mobilization of the company's resources, her marketing skills, her negotiating skills, and her perseverance. Although all these things do play a crucial role in business dynamics, Jing Ma failed to assess the other players involved in the business deal. After looking at the bigger picture, it became clear that because of Giant's merger with Stop & Shop, buyers were hesitant to take a risk with a new product.

This was especially true with limited shelf space in a popular and highly competitive category such as frozen foods. If, instead of counting solely on her abilities, Jing Ma had analyzed the complete picture and been more proficient with assessing the situations of all the stakeholders, she would have recognized that the strategy she had adopted wasn't going to work. She could have saved Jammin' Foods valuable time and money. Ultimately, she may have never even pursued the Giant opportunity but instead invested Jammin's resources on a different opportunity that had a better chance of a favorable outcome.

The lessons from this failure paint a classic scenario where the bravado and ego of one individual trying to land the big fish tied up the limited resources of a start-up. In my experience as a consultant to dozens and dozens of start-up companies, I am asked to solve the problems created by these kinds of ego-driven strategies all the time.

You will never read a business self-help book entitled *Ten Steps to Gaining Humility,* or a magazine article called "Put Humility Back in Your Life: Here's How!" You can't get credit for a course in humility in any business school that I know of. You learn humility as result of the business experiences you encounter and how you react to these outcomes along the way. In other words, you don't develop humility; it develops you.

Hang around long enough in any business situation, and you are bound to get kicked, stomped on, chopped up, or booted out. This is just the nature of business, where one minute you are today's hero and the next you are the scapegoat. Strap the next building band on: humility.

CHAPTER 6

Failure Is an Option: Flying Fear in Formation

In April 1970, when things went wrong aboard the Apollo 13 spacecraft, astronaut Jim Lovell told Mission Control, "Houston, we've got a problem." In response to the challenge of coming up with a solution to the spacecraft's near-fatal problems, Gene Kranz, the lead flight director for Mission Control, told his team. "Failure is not an option."

Kranz's words were immortalized in the 1995 movie *Apollo 13,* and this phrase has now become the rallying cry for many a sports team and corporation. Unfortunately, these words don't hold up in life and especially not in business, where failure is almost always an option.

We don't need stargazing or a crystal ball to figure this out. Failure is in each of our futures somewhere and probably in most of our pasts, where it likely has appeared more than once. If you say you have never met failure and never will, then you are either not being honest or you have simply set your goals too low.

Statistically, failure is the most likely business outcome we all face as most companies fail after five years. Larry Farrell in *Across the Board* magazine states that out of 100 people, 70 will want to start a business, 15 will actually do so in the next few years, and only 5 will succeed on the first try.[1] In business, this makes failure far more common than success.

Greet Failure with a New Vocabulary

In case you have not met in a while, let me reintroduce you to failure. Failure is brassy, never shy. Failure is red, never yellow or green. Failure is a good teacher but a bad learner. Failure prefers dim light. Failure's favorite time of year is winter. Failure is like fire, a bruise, ice, and chili peppers.

Scott Sandage, professor at Carnegie Mellon University and author of *Born Losers* (Harvard University Press, 2005), says that "we're so attuned to the possibilities of success that we don't have the vocabulary for talking about failure. That's why we have catch-all words like *loser*."[2]

We learn this at an early age. I can still picture my younger son and his friends forming an L with their thumbs and forefingers and waving their hands above their heads to make fun of a team that lost. As adults, the expressions we use to describe failure are even more severe and hurtful: *botch, bust, decay, deadbeat, derelict, deficiency, dud, fiasco, good for nothing, loafer, moocher, nobody, sinking ship, washout,* and *wreck*.

Not a pretty picture. Words like these denote someone who is broke and lazy, someone who has something inherently wrong with them. In Yiddish, someone who fails is called a *nebbish*—literally, a nothing. The language we use does influence the way we feel and how we will act next, and words like *botch, bust, nebbish,* and *failure* have tremendous power to make us feel horrible.

To grow true business confidence for ourselves and for the people around us, we must rethink our vocabulary, and stop using failure as a label for so many things. If we are ever going to achieve true business confidence, we must invest more in clearly understanding the cause and effect of an undesired and unexpected outcome, rather than simply dismiss it with the word *failure*.

Learning to call failure something neutral, like *decision point, outcome,* or *result* helps develop bounce. Scott Jordan, founder of Scottevest, also believes that the words we use are important. "Without some failures, you cannot have success. Every successful venture involves failures. Given that, I prefer not to use the term *failure*. It is an ugly and definitive word and it implies an ending point. Rather, I use the term *disappointment*; it is not as scary or definitive."

Anna Belyaev, CEO of Type A, a training agency, takes a very long view in judging her business life's success and failure. "I try to stick to a very objective definition of failure. At the end of the day what I usually say is you don't know whether you fail until you're dead."

She makes a good point. Why not let others struggle with labeling our results as failure or success after we are gone? As former American president Bill Clinton said, "Defeat is never final"[3]

Meet Failure's Close Relative, Fear

No matter what vocabulary we use, no matter how much business confidence we manage to develop (crazy or otherwise), it's a fact of life and business that we are all afraid of failure sometimes. Fear is not brought on by our competitors or outside forces. It mostly originates within us, and when fear becomes the director of our daily business life it is paralyzing.

I laugh when I see popular T-shirts that say we should not be afraid of failure. There is an American clothing company called No Fear. SoBe has a "No Fear" drink. Nissan brings us a "No Fear" Titan truck. There is even an American television show called *Fear Factor*, where contestants need to deal with their fear in order to win.

Fear may sell consumer products and commercial air time, but in business this whistling-in-the-dark attitude is all nonsense and only provides a false bravado, a hollow rallying cry that no one really listens to and which only holds us back from progressing forward along our path. We don't get anywhere by denying our fear. We have to learn to accept it and make it work for us.

And sometimes there is absolutely nothing wrong with this fear—in fact, it makes good sense. When I first started studying karate, one of the well-known guidelines at the school, which I eventually wrote down in my journal, was "Fear? See Sensei Sarah." The leaders of the karate school knew that instead of denying fear, we should deal with it. Sensei Sarah was the one who would help when it came up for every member.

Collin Anderson knew a lot about fear even before he went into business for himself. He created the Skip Doctor product to clean CDs and DVDs and sold millions of copies. He agrees that we all fear failure. Here's what he told me:

> Fear of failure holds a lot of people back. We all fear it. Nobody wants to be embarrassed. When I was kid, I admired the undefeated team. To me, that was the ultimate. To win and never lose was my goal. As I've grown older, I've changed my thinking. I admire those who have been down in the mud. It inoculates you for the future. If you've ever played football in the snow and the rain, initially, you are tentative. You don't want to get dirty. Once you do, you revel in the pure freedom. It's fun. There is some of that with starting up a business, too. Just to know that you've been through it. It's a factor in being more secure. That you don't fear it anymore.

Fear of Being Different and Not as Successful as I Ought to Be

Fear of failure has many levels. As businesspeople, we are afraid of disappointing customers, partners, team members, bosses, board members, or shareholders. We are afraid we will lose business, get fired, or go bankrupt. We are afraid of disappointing our friends and our family. In fact, at a deep level, we know that this is inevitable—since other people get to set their own expectations of us and they get to assess our seeming failures against their own measuring stick. The only expectation and assessment that we control is our own.

Selina Kucks, who owns a ballet school in Australia, points out what she believes is the source of our fear: "Eighty-five percent of the battle in anyone's life is fear of being different, being rejected for being different, and what others will think if you do not succeed. These thoughts are also what plagues every entrepreneur who has ever had ideas of going it alone in the world of business."[4]

Inside many of us, alongside the fear of being different is the fear that someone else in our position would have done the job better. The deepest fear for many businesspeople is not actually failing (probably because it is so hard for us to admit that the possibility to fail exists); rather, it is being less successful than we think we ought to be or than our mothers, our bosses, or society expect us to be.

This is exactly Manish Patel's fear. As the 10-year CEO of Where2GetIt, he has built a very successful and profitable company. But he has a lot of self-doubt since he believes that someone else in his shoes would have done things better and achieved a superior result. "They would have made better decisions than me and would have built it faster and more profitably than I did." For many of us, the main attack on our confidence is from this unlikely source. We believe that we should be in a different place than where we are right now, and that we would be, if only we had made better decisions.

Fight this. It is your insecurity talking. You could not have made any different judgments than you did at that moment in time, and you must learn to accept this as fact. You were at a certain point and, given all that you knew, you made the best decision to achieve the most successful outcome that you knew how to make.

The Elements Called Success and Failure

Similar to the idea that love and hate are very close together on the circle of passion, success and failure are neighbors as well, as depicted in Figure 6.1.

Figure 6.1 Chart of Success and Failure

This is why the way that we define failure and the perspective from which we look at it influence us. A short-term success can actually be a failure, while some things that can be viewed as failures are actually viewed as successes later on. A business friend of mine came in third for windsurfing in an effort to qualify for the Olympics. He failed to be an Olympic athlete. Instead, he succeeded in starting a business in the 1990s that he ended up selling for millions of dollars. Success or failure; you tell me.

With true business confidence, you realize that success and failure are a matter of perspective and of definition. How we use these two angles can influence how we feel. Our mental perspective has a huge effect on how we approach things and what we do next.

In one of the best scenes from one of my favorite movies, *Ferris Buehler's Day Off*, the intrepid main character wants to eat at a very fancy and snooty Chicago restaurant. When the maitre d' refuses to seat him, Ferris tries five different approaches, finally succeeding by faking a telephone call to himself implying that he is Abe Froeman, the sausage king of Chicago.

This is a common situation that many of us have had to face. It illustrates that it helps to have thought through several plans so that we are prepared regardless of what result occurs. Knowing what we will do next after the action either succeeds or fails is empowering enough to catapult us to a place that offers an opportunity to succeed the next time around.

FUD Takes Hold

Fear holds us back from many things in business. James Waldroop, a business psychologist and former director of MBA career development programs at the Harvard Business School, says that "The enemy of a good decision is fear—fear of failure, fear of humiliation, fear of making a mistake."[5]

When I was employed at IBM in the 1980s, we had a saying that no one ever got fired for buying IBM. In those days, we had to sell against other competitors whose products were less expensive and probably often comparable technologically. Fortunately for me and my peers, the technical manager (back when it was called *data processing*) many times chose IBM despite the fact that we were more expensive, because we were the low-risk alternative. By buying a proven brand, even if it cost more, the manager could justify his decision as a good one.

As an IBM marketing manager, I used a technique that we internally called FUD (fear, uncertainty, and doubt) to direct the technical manager's decision-making process my way. I recounted all the things that could go wrong if he chose a vendor other than IBM. This FUD technique typically worked.

We are sometimes trained not to make a mistake rather than to take chances that can win for us. This can lead to diminished or detrimental outcomes, and sometimes our very fear of failure actually provides the most direct route to failing. With so much focus on the possibility of failing, we meet our expectations and fail.

Pamela Slim, an entrepreneur in Arizona, wrote a work manifesto for her blog, "Escape from Cubicle Nation," about fear. She declares that "fear is the great inhibitor. All of the excuses that you find for not doing work you love have solutions. You do not enact them because you are afraid: of showing up too big in the world; of failing; of appearing as an imposter; of living in poverty. There is nothing wrong with fear. Feel it, talk to it, examine it, and walk with it. Then step out and let yourself show up, warts and all. It will liberate you."[6]

Sometimes in sports, when a team is far ahead in the score, they back off and play it safe with the lesser goal of not losing, instead of playing to win. This actually gives their losing opponents an opportunity to come back since the losing team will play more aggressively and take more chances, because as losers they have nothing more to lose. This is classically what happens when teams that are very far behind in the score come back to win.

Before my children were born, I played a lot of golf. Correct that—I played a lot of *bad* golf because I always thought I looked stupid swinging the club. I was most afraid of placing a bad shot into the bunker or sand trap because I knew that I lacked the skill to recover, and once the ball went in the sand, it would be nearly impossible for me to get it out.

When I was on the fairway, I kept thinking, "I hope I do not hit the ball into the sand trap because I will never get it out!" With all that focus on *not* hitting the ball into the sand trap, guess where

I almost always hit it? I went straight to the beach. I got never got much good at using a sand wedge, although I had a lot of practice. I am—in golf at least—walking proof of Earl Nightingale's famous motivational quote, "You are what you think about."

Skip the Logo Design, Take a Step

Nick Papadopoulos has a client whose fear of moving forward in her business spelled her ultimate failure. Nick explains, "She spent all her time thinking about things she had to do to be prepared—pricing structure, business cards, and the office. By the time she got all those things, she was broke." It's good to have all those things when you build a business, but if you keep waiting to be perfectly prepared for anything that can go wrong, your business is never going to happen.

When I started my first deals, I didn't have a business card, a tax ID number, pricing structure, or even a company name. After I got one client, I got others, and then I started to add those operational things. Out of ugliness and uncertainly can come really good stuff. The best visions for a business are the ones that develop out of talking to customers rather than those you write into the business plan.

When you are in the start-up game, by the very nature of it, you have to spend less time trying to anticipate every possible nuance and more time taking actions based on the belief that somehow you are going to be able to get from where you are to where you want to be. You don't know exactly how, but you have to have the confidence (or sometimes bluff or bravado) to believe that there is a path.

Most people who talk about starting a business, as Larry Farrell's statistics indicate, never carry out their plan. The possibility of actually going forward and asking prospective customers to buy your product is so much more daunting than sitting in front of your computer planning to start a company. Customers might say no, and the fear of rejection is too great for many of us. This is an extension of the fear that we may not live up to others' expectations.

Fear of Failure Can Motivate, and
Then It's Not All Bad

Failure can be so uncomfortable that sometimes the fear of failure actually propels us to push forward. Many times in business, the only thing that made me move was the greater fear that staying exactly where I was would never lead to success or, worse, would hasten my failure. I knew I needed to do something different because whatever I was doing was not working and I could not figure out why. Staying in the same place would in all probability lead to the same results. Moving by taking another action or tactic would produce a different result and I would at least have another opportunity to achieve the successful outcome I wanted.

JD Wetherspoon is one of the most successful restaurant chains in Britain. Its founder, Tim Martin, named these pubs for one of his teachers in New Zealand who suggested that Tim would never amount to anything. With 650 establishments in his business, I guess he has finally showed that teacher that he was wrong.

Rick Mazursky, who ran VTech Toys and then Digital Innovations, which manufactures the Skip Doctor (invented by Collin Anderson), says that he learned to keep on moving in basic training in the military. "Our first day of bayonet training, they told us that there are only two kinds of people in this world: the quick and the dead."

As a dancer, Linda Regulbuto says that there is no such thing as true balance. "If you are completely balanced, you are dead. Even when a dancer is on one toe, she is moving. It's called the candy cane effect. To the audience, you look perfectly still but inside you are moving side to side just to keep your balance." Like a dancer, in business, you are never really in balance. You are either riding the wave or getting washed up on the beach. That's why fear can be good—it can propel you move to another place. Fear makes focusing a necessity.

Facing Your Fear: Jump!

Fear is good. It is natural and organic. I got to take a close look at fear when I traveled to Queenstown, New Zealand, on vacation with my family. In this place, you can bungee jump off of bridges, swing into vast canyons, jump out of airplanes, ski from helicopters, and fly gliders. This popular tourist city is widely known as the "Extreme Sports Capital of the World."

After visiting it, I call it the "Extreme Fear Capital of the World." Why do tourists come here to do the scariest physical things possible that they would never, ever do in daily life? Why do they challenge themselves to such extremes?

At Shotover Canyon Swing, Harry Cutler straps harnesses onto the visitors and prepares people to jump 150 meters into a canyon. He has helped people face their fear of dropping into the river-filled ravine every day for the past three years. Cutler has strapped 10,000 people into harnesses to do their freefall jump, and he says that people actually never overcome their fear of jumping. They are afraid—and do it anyway. He says that he has personally jumped 300 times and each time he is *still* afraid even though he knows exactly what is going on. The scariest moment of his career was when he saw his mother jump!

According to Harry, when jumpers approach the platform after having paid over $100, they all say the same thing: "I can't jump" or "I've changed my mind, I don't want to jump." He looks at the person's body language to see what they are really saying. If they are shaking violently, then they may have some real issues; otherwise, Harry says he tries to act as mentor and get them to trust him. They proceed to try to talk themselves out of jumping. Harry has heard everything as he stares his customers' fear literally in the face every day.

Mostly, Harry tells people not to look down before they jump and to just face whatever happens on the way down instead of overthinking what will happen. Good advice, Harry, I thought when he told me this. Good advice in many parts of our lives, and especially in business.

Most things that we fear actually never happen. We spend more time being afraid of being afraid then actually experiencing true fear. Sometimes it takes people 30 minutes on Harry's platform to take the jump. Interestingly enough, once people decide not to jump and get off the platform, almost none of them ever return for a second chance.

Harry believes people jump for the bragging rights. Photo and video sales of their jumps are very high. People see it as an accomplishment. He is not sure if people really enjoy the jump, but it is exhilarating. He thinks they use it as a way of compensating for fears they are unable to face in their everyday life.

Fortunately, a warning sign in front of the canyon site listed various medical conditions with which you could not jump. Luckily, I qualified for a few. I watched my wife jump. Having known her for almost 20 years, I though I had seen her exhibit every emotion possible, from laughing to crying to screaming. When she jumped, she let out a primal grunt that I had never heard come from her mouth. On the fear scale, what comes before screaming for my wife is this grunting as she braced herself for the fall.

Why do we jump off a bungee platform or take risks in business? What are we trying to prove to ourselves or to others? Do we need to face this fear so we can face other fears in our life? Do we jump because we want to lose control since we are forced to have so much in control in our regular life?

Bungee jumping is similar to those times in business when we try to face things we are afraid to do. Some people say that we need to face fear to get past it. Some say we need to embrace fear. I say, don't always look before you jump, as long as you can handle what comes after you jump, whether it is the rush of adrenaline, the glow of victory, the blow of bust, or the agony of bankruptcy.

Teaching Butterflies to Fly in Formation

When I was at IBM, I took a few Dale Carnegie classes. One of the best things that I learned was how to harness the fear of failure. We have all had that strange feeling in our stomach that happens to us before we do something where we are afraid. We characterized it as "butterflies in our stomach." Wisely, the Dale Carnegie class did not teach me techniques to eliminate that fear. It taught me to teach the butterflies to fly in formation.

The actual fear of failure can grow less severe, but it never completely goes away. In fact, eliminating fear is unrealistic and unproductive. There are many good reasons to be afraid. Using our fears and teaching them to fly in formation will produce the best outcome. It might not be perfect; it might even be failure—but it will be the best possible outcome for that set of circumstances at that point in time.

Speaking in front of audiences is a common fear. It is even said that people are more afraid of speaking in front of an audience than they are of death. In other words, the quip goes, "Most people would rather be dead then be standing in front of you today."

I am often asked if I ever get nervous when I speak in front of large audiences. I *always* get nervous. But this type of nervous fear is good—it is part of my process, and I have learned to use it to my advantage. It increases my energy level, heightens my senses, and gets me ready to speak as if I were doing it for the very first time.

I use many techniques to get my fear of speaking to fly in formation. Before I speak, I try to meet the people who will be listening to me, so that they are not a faceless, scary crowd. Later, it helps to look out at them and be able to connect with a familiar, friendly face. As I meet them, I give out my "GET CRAZY" buttons to lessen the tension, get some early laughs, and begin to bond with the audience.

But still, after I am introduced, as I make my way to the stage, the butterflies are still raging in my stomach. When the polite applause ends, I make a point to start every speech with the same five sentences that always get a laugh from the audience. These are words that I have practiced thousands of times. This enables me, in front of the bright lights and a new audience, to execute the credibility-building part of the speech perfectly. I can then relax and quickly get those who are listening on my side. The rest of the speech becomes much easier.

This is one of the ways that experience and effort bring order to the butterflies. I don't wish *not* to be afraid when I go up on stage. This fear, when the butterflies are flying in formation, actually powers my energy to connect to the audience because they are such an important component for a successful speech.

I am also afraid of flying. Although I board an airplane more than 100 times a year, I am scared. If I am so afraid, why do I get on the jet? Because what is waiting on the other side—speaking to business, academic, and economic organizations—gives me so much passion and joy. If I don't fly to them, I don't get to experience what I really enjoy.

I have learned the only way to deal with the fear of flying is to channel it into something else. But how do I get through the bad airplane turbulence (like I am experiencing right now as I edit this page)? I have learned to use high-energy music on my iPod to redirect all the airplane bumps. I use a play list called "Turbulence Tunes" to channel the bumps in the air into dancing in my seat.

I face my fear of failure every day now that I have had diabetes for over 10 years. Every day I am tested—literally. I medically test my blood sugar at least four times a day to see if it is in the seemingly impossible normal range of 80 to 120.

Many mornings, I fail to be in that range. I feel shame and try to remember what I did wrong the day before—too much food, not enough insulin, or too little exercise. I feel bad when I fail this morning test because blood sugar results outside the normal range contribute to health complications and an early demise. But I've learned that I have to move on past this test, adjust my insulin, eat, and see if I can pass the test in three hours before my next meal

With Failure and Fear Comes Choice

Joshua Piven, author of *As Luck Would Have It: Incredible Stories from Lottery Wins to Lightning Strikes,* writes that what people fear is really the absence of control.[7] Larry Cunningham, an entrepreneur who runs Corepole, an exercise equipment company, says that he is driven by the fear that he has so much money and time invested in his business that he has no choice but to keep going.

But there is always a choice, if you are willing to recognize it. There are times when you realize that you must go in a different direction with your business. Colin Jones describes it as a point where "You've come to a halt, period. You're powerless to keep things going in the direction you want them to go."

The fact is, in almost every case, we have choices. Fear may paralyze us so we do not recognize the choices, but they are always there if we pause to look at the decision-making process. We always have the choice to keep doing what we are doing or to stop and do something else. Stopping is many times the more difficult choice. Choice is an antidote to fear. It doesn't get rid of it, but it allows us to live with it.

Even when I failed, I never went hungry. My family has never been without a place to live. I have always found a way to put food on the table and hopefully always will. This may seem obvious, but it is something we need to remember when we have failed and have a very low opinion of our prospects for the future. In fact, what I am most proud of in my life is that I can financially support my family (so far) doing something that I enjoy doing. This, to me, is the biggest miracle of all.

Facing the fear of failure by *recognizing you always have a choice* is the third building band for true business confidence. Failure is an option, and so is fear. It is okay to be afraid. Teach those butterflies in your stomach to fly in formation by facing what needs to come next, over and over again. It does not matter if someone else would have done it differently or better. This is *your* life. Practice and iteration help. Jump if you can handle the outcome no matter what it is.

The key is to understand that it is okay to be afraid—we all are—and then to go ahead and push forward any way. As my attorney, Zane Smith, always told me when things were going badly for me, "Remember, the worst they can do is eat you, and that is illegal."

CHAPTER 7

Embracing Failure When It Happens

It is a daunting paradox. Countries and cultures around the world believe that Americans are lucky in business since we are allowed to fail. Financially and legally, we *are* given second and third chances. For the most part, when we fail and go out of business, we are not sent to prison for the money that our corporation owes (thanks to the corporate rules that make a company a separate entity from its owner).

It is commonly expressed in American business culture that it is okay to fail. Sometimes our culture even seems to insist that it is necessary to fail in order to be successful, because we learn so much from those failures. Hence, you get book titles such as Joey Green's *The Road to Success Is Paved with Failure* (Little, Brown and Company, 2001), which paints portraits of all the failures that famous people have overcome.

But there is an important caveat accompanying this idea that it is okay to fail: It is okay to fail as long as failure isn't the last thing that happens. In other words, if a success follows, then failure was okay. But if there is no follow-on success, failure is seen as a black, dark pit.

This is why archetype three—try harder—has become such a mantra in American business culture. When Americans fail, we tell ourselves stories to make us feel better. When it rains on a bride's wedding day, we say that this is good luck. (Too bad if her parents had to move the wedding indoors). When a bird poops on us, we call that good luck, too. (Never mind that it smells bad and stains our shirt.)

Failure is not a prerequisite to success. When we fail, sometimes we don't learn anything. Many times, failure has absolutely nothing to teach us, and we fail for no apparent useful reason. Why do we hide failure, if it is touted in our classrooms and motivational business books as being such a necessary component of success? If our culture really thinks that failure is an essential ingredient for success, then when we fail we should be sending e-mails to all the people in our business network that read something like this:

To: Everyone I Know

From: Barry Moltz

Subject: Yippee! Another Failure

I can't help but brag that I have failed yet again. I am writing because I knew you would want to share this wonderful moment with me. I am so proud of myself because as a result of my latest failure and all the unbelievable things I was able to learn, I am now so much closer to that big financial success I deserve. I am certain that my time is coming soon since I have failed at an increasing rate lately, and I have learned so much. Please stay in touch so I can share with you when I have an even greater failure and get that much closer to the success you all want for me.

Your close business friend,

Barry

It is unlikely that you will ever send or receive an e-mail like this—even from me. Instead, when failure comes our way, we typically burrow deep into our hole. That hiding actually becomes the hardest part. For those of us who have failed (like me), we hide because we feel ashamed. We want to see failure as a necessary step toward success, but that's hard to do when we are in the middle of a terrible episode—and besides, it might not be true.

One of the most painful and sudden apparent failures I have ever witnessed in sports was Adam Greenberg in his first and only time at bat with the Chicago Cubs. On July 9, 2005, Greenberg was hit in the head by Florida Marlins pitcher Valerio de los Santos on the very first and only pitch that was ever thrown to him in major league baseball.

He went down with a concussion and never returned to the game that day. For that matter, Greenberg has never played major league baseball again. Is this a failure on his part or just bad luck? What can he learn from this failure—that when a rock-hard ball is thrown at you at 100 mph you should duck?

If we only look at the outcome, Greenberg failed. He failed to get a hit (although his team did get to put a man on base, thanks to a strange rule of baseball that when you get hit by the pitcher, you are able to walk to first base). But did Greenberg really fail as a batter, even though he had no real control over the outcome?

One could argue that he failed to get out of the way of the ball, or that he failed to have a head hard enough to protect him from a concussion. Or did the pitcher fail by hitting him? Or did the manufacturer of the batter's helmet fail because it did not protect Greenberg's head? The outcome is that as a result of this incident, Greenberg is still in the minor leagues, and still has not reached his goal of playing major league baseball.

Failure is not the necessary prerequisite to success some think it to be. Some people do succeed without painful failure. This actually further confuses us and causes us to hide failure even more. If we are really truthful and assess the situation accurately, many times a failure does nothing to contribute to our overall goal of success. In reality, the actual failure really wasn't part of the path to success; it was more like a rest stop or a detour to a not-so-nice place for no reason at all.

Reverse-Engineering Our Past

The positive impact that many failures have on our success often comes about in the retelling of our personal business stories after we have become very successful. It makes our own road-to-success tale just that much more magical. To survive in a business culture and hide any shame we have about failure, we go back and reengineer things as success and failure after the fact to fit our specific needs.

Many of us, like Bruce Zamost, a product liability attorney in New Jersey, do not remember personal failures clearly. Bruce says, "Each of my victories has been elevated to the level of historical fact, to be retold to my legacy, in 'big fish' fashion. Each of my failures has been minimized to tadpoles."

In *Fooled by Randomness* (Random House, 2005, second ed.), Nassim Nicholas Taleb writes that "past events always look less random than they were (it is called hindsight bias). I would listen to someone's discussion of his own past realizing that much of what he was saying was just the back-fit explanations concocted ex post by his deluded mind."

Many times in retelling our story, we attribute our disproportionate share of good luck to something else, perhaps intelligence or skill. But with true business confidence, we do not need to reverse-engineer our failures. We can invest our energy into moving forward rather than reinventing the past.

Oh, What a Shame

Failure is defined in the Oxford English Dictionary as "deficient or inadequate." *Shame* is defined as "guilt, embarrassment, unworthiness, disgrace, and dishonor." Yes, yes, yes, yes, and yes. There is a good reason that the dictionary does not define failure as "something that leads to success."

Since we are conditioned early on to succeed by our parents and by the archetypes of success in a highly competitive world, shame is thrust upon us when our result is something that can be easily defined as failure. Most of us ingest it wholeheartedly, but we should not accept the shame thrust upon us by others too readily.

We actually don't want to look at people who are going through failure except at a distance, and then our thoughts often are more about how we are glad *they* are going through it, not us, rather than about what we could learn from the situation. Hardly anyone wants to hear about failure when it is going on, and no one wants to be associated with it when it is happening.

Nicolas Hall, former president of the Silicon Valley Association of Startup Entrepreneurs, founded a web site called Startupfailures.com, where he discussed the entrepreneurial life. The site had a community of experts but eventually was unable to get venture capital funding. He explained that while they acknowledged that failure was the best teacher for future success, the venture capitalists were reluctant to be associated with the "failure piece of the journey."

Until I had sold my third business successfully during the Internet bubble, there wasn't a single person (including my mother) who wanted to hear my story of going out of business and then being kicked out of my next business. As the expression goes, "Success has many fathers, but failure is an orphan." Once I really understood this, I realized that my business confidence could not come from just my successful outcomes or what other people thought of those outcomes—I had to find a way to give failure a role.

It is a much better story to say that we came from *nothing* and made *something* of our life than it is to start with something and go to nothing. (Those archetypes again!) We like the underdog story because we can visualize ourselves in the starring role, especially at times when things are going poorly. These stories fit the archetype of "Failure and hard work lead to success," giving us something to hold on to when things seem hopeless.

Even though U.S. culture gives lip service to the idea that it's okay to fail, businesses actually want people who fail to hide their failures and then their heads. We only want to see them when they have made amends and produced a follow-on success so that they can now tell the underdog story of how they came back from the brink of extinction to find success.

As businesspeople, when we fail, we accept the shame and guilt because, regardless of how the business or situation ended, we feel responsible. Even though many of us are too quick to take sole responsibility for what is labeled a failure, no matter what happened or what actually caused these events, somewhere in the deep recesses of our character, we believe it was our fault.

It is easy to see why many businesspeople feel shame. We think, like Andria Lieu, that if only we had made different decisions, failure could have been avoided. We are embarrassed because we promised those around us a different outcome, and now we have to admit that we were wrong. We feel unworthy and less than what we were or had hoped to be. Somehow we have brought dishonor and disgrace to ourselves, to our family, and to others who associate with us.

Is there ever a benefit to feeling shame? As with everything, it depends. Start by learning the difference between feeling *shame* and being *ashamed*. A person should feel ashamed if they have truly done something wrong. Feeling ashamed is a useful tool, if we use those feelings as a way to alert us to bad behavior that we want to stop.

If you overbilled your client, be ashamed. If you sold a customer a bad product, be ashamed. Humility has enabled me to make amends for things I have done that I am ashamed of in business. However, it isn't helpful to feel ashamed if we did our best to get a successful outcome with the best intentions and fell flat on our face (or some other part of our anatomy). Grieving is okay, even necessary—failure is, after all, a kind of loss. Pause to feel it. Beat yourself up; cry and wallow. Declare all woe to you if this makes you feel better. Feel whatever you need to feel, and then get past it.

Although responsibility is important, sometimes the ego makes us take things much too personally. When I have felt shame in my failures, I have thought many times that the best solution would be to tie myself to my computer and take a shower. This would achieve the contrition I needed and provide me the relief from shame I was looking for through my version of self-electrocution.

Kevin Turner of Modelmetrics says that when we experience failure, we need to let the body "metabolize and pass it." With this imagery we can visualize what it is like for the body to first wallow and absorb the failure and then eventually move on to another place.

When we act in an honest and forthright manner with maximum effort, whatever shame or grief we feel can be temporary. The key is to accept failure without shame, so that we can learn humility (building band 2) from either failure or success.

Forgive Others—And Then Yourself

Gail Blanke, author of *Between Trapezes* (Rodale Books, 2004), writes that the biggest thing she has learned is how to be a great editor in her life. "You have to edit out not only those voices, but also the stuff that didn't work. Trapeze artists have a saying, 'The greatest fliers are the greatest fallers.' Trapeze artists never confuse falling with failing. You've got people that just keep reinventing themselves, what they do, and reinventing the way they do it, and we believe in them." If you can figure out in your own profession how not to confuse falling with failing, you won't feel shame, you will achieve true confidence

Blanke believes if you present yourself with clarity like Donald Trump, Cher, Madonna, and Hillary Clinton, people will be drawn to you. She believes we need to distinguish between fact and interpretation of why we failed.

"If they don't call you back, you could let it mean that you're not that good, versus some other interpretation, like they're out of town, or they're taking their company in an entirely different direction. In other words, it's about them, not me. . . . We diminish ourselves by placing negative interpretations on the stuff that happens in our lives. Keep deleting the failures, deleting the fears and deleting whatever you consider your mistakes.

This is not the same as the reverse engineering previously discussed. This is making adjustments in our outlook, attitude, and viewpoint in real time to set up for the next best possible outcome.

When I worked at larger corporations, one of the most useless activities that we did after a group failure was to sit around and figure out who was to blame. This was not the same as discussing what actually went wrong as a way to do things better the next time. This was a process that bogged the group down in blame.

Don't do this—not to yourself and not to other people, either. I am not suggesting that we shouldn't accept responsibility for our actions, but we need to forgive ourselves for everything that we were able to do and what we were not able to do in any particular situation. Holding on to blame only impedes our next efforts to be successful and chips away at our bounce. Blame makes a person feel like a loser.

Adopt this mantra: I am not my business. I am not my business. A failed business or failed event does not make me a failure.

Moving Outcomes: Owning Our Mistakes

How do we take ownership for our mistakes without wallowing in shame? By accepting and learning to recognize how each experience, positive or negative, has value in helping us decide what to do next.

We can spend some time figuring out our part in every mistake and perhaps what others contributed as well. Many times the forces beyond our control (and yes, there are many) play a part in the mistake. In total the universe may not make mistakes. What is supposed to happen happens with a sort of natural flow and consequence, and in the interest of that big picture, sometimes some of us have to fail.

Each outcome is like randomly climbing or descending the stairs. Your particular goal may be at the top or the bottom of the stairs. It may be to the side at one particular landing. Treat all the outcomes you label "failure" with an open mind and appreciative attitude, and learn from them. When we are finally able to let go, we are ready for the next experience.

The fourth major building band of true business confidence is to *give up the shame*. When you fail, feel shame if you must, and if you need to, grieve. Deflect the shame that others cast upon you. Ideally, never feel shame if you acted in a rightful manner. Shame only gets in the way since it has a tendency to stick to us and everything around us. Shame only strengthens the ego to act. It does not provide the basis for a healthy balance of humility. Let the shame fade so you can move on to whatever comes next.

This Thing We Call Failure

So what exactly is considered failure? This is interesting to consider since we do the categorization of failure after the fact—at the point of outcome. A failure can be many things. It could be a result of an oversight, a mistake, or an accident. It could be a result of an act of a higher being or a natural disaster. It could be result of a miscalculation or an error in judgment.

In downhill skiing for the Olympics, being slower by a fraction of a second could mean missing out on the gold medal—a failure, certainly. Alternately, since I had a hard time walking correctly as a child, success could mean meeting my goal of finishing running the marathon in under four hours as I did in 1984. Success could be surviving when you are lost in the wilderness or when you are lost in the mall.

Success and failure as outcomes really belong on a continuum, but we tend to consider them as stand-alone events. While this after-the-fact, black-and-white definition may make categorizing an event easier, we lose the opportunity to gain resiliency, confidence, and good process. We would be better served by channeling the energy that we direct at labeling outcomes back into looking at the process that got us there.

Wally Amos, who was a talent agent before he created the Famous Amos cookie empire, gives a new meaning to the word *mistake*:

> During the 14 years I was in show business, I went to many recording sessions. Each time a song is recorded, that's called a "take." Let's say you do 90 takes. Everyone who's involved in that effort listens closely to Take 90. They do not condemn, judge, or criticize, because everyone is listening for ways to make take 90 a better take. Then they go back into the control room and do take 91. So take 90 was just a "mis-take."[1]

Embracing Failure: An Acquired Taste

My start in business was with IBM at age 21, two weeks after I graduated from college, and I did not fail a lot for the first nine years of my professional life. Success at IBM came fairly easy as their rules of business engagement were straightforward, there was a proven framework of support, and the company was committed to training all employees extremely well. For their first year at IBM, all new sales and technical branch office hires were sent to internal schools on the products, the competition, and the company culture—almost everything a salesperson or systems engineer would need to know to sell and install mainframe hardware and software systems.

The methods of success at IBM were an extension of the ones that I had learned in school: Listen and learn from what your teachers were telling you and, for the most part, do what you were told. Observe how others succeeded before you, and follow that proven and well-traveled path.

When I left the IBM cocoon in 1990 to go work for my own clients, failure slapped me on the side of the head so many times that I almost lost count. The young and aggressive company where I went to work had a totally different set of rules for success.

We got ahead by being friendly with the owner. We got ahead by dressing in designer clothes. We got ahead by ratting out people who were disloyal to the owner. We got ahead only if we were successful when we took risks, and then only if the owner could take credit for our success When I began to realize all of this, I felt like I had parachuted into a foreign country.

I became business road kill as my misadventures started to accumulate. Finally the owner fired me. I then decided that after being too confined by other businesspeople's rules, I would start my own company in the advertising business, although I knew little about it. The rules here were even more foreign, and with no administrative support structure and no marketing brand, I was out of business in six months.

I am not sure that we are responsible for our business success and failure as much as we are there as a participant to ride the business through its own series of good and bad times. We are not so much like the driver of a car, but more like bull riders who try to stay in the saddle long enough to beat the eight-second clock. We don't really take business where we want it to go as much as we guide it as it takes us.

I am not saying that we don't influence outcomes; we do, and better executives, owners, and managers have better influence. But it's more like sailing, where you have your hand on the rudder as you direct the boat through the water, than it is like being the conductor leading an orchestra.

When charting your course by compass, if you change your direction slightly, over the long term you will end up in a very different place. It's often like that in business. Sometimes, all you need to do is turn a business five degrees from its current heading to achieve the financial success you seek; sometimes two degrees the other way will cause a business to fail.

We might be able to go through life without any scars at all. If a pin prick could get our attention the same way as getting stabbed in the back with a butcher's knife, who wouldn't opt for the pin? But if multiple scars are necessary, at least they do become less deep and painful as they accumulate. Scars not only toughen the skin, but amazingly they also improve your hearing and sharpen your eyesight.

When I fail now, I just fail. For sure I feel sorrow and usually shame—at least initially. I have the tendency to wallow in it, which is the part that I especially love. I am still my mother's son, after all. But that part of my cycle doesn't last as long as it used to—maybe a day, or at most a week or two of bad dreams if it is a huge business loss. Then I move on, and I am in a better position to handle the fear of whatever comes next.

Like Success, Failure Is Part of the Cycle of Business

But something is different for me now than 10 or 20 years ago. I no longer look for helpful bandages or sympathy to smooth over my wounds so they will heal correctly. Rather, I see my experiences as just another part of the business cycle.

It is easy to use past successes to bolster confidence and as encouragement to expect future success. But I now know how to use my failures the same way—to remember that although I failed before and probably will again, it doesn't make *me* a failure. I have failed after I failed, failed after I succeeded, and succeeded after I failed. Any of these outcomes can and likely will come again—and there is no way to predict which will arrive first.

Kara Trott, president of Quantum Health Corporation, believes that the way the owner reacts to failure sets a tone for the entire company. "Start with picking yourself up, dusting yourself off, say, 'Oh well,' and move on. Be an adult; get over it. You have to ask yourself, 'What did I learn?' Just move on, very quickly—like, in a day. You can't wallow, you have to come back and lead your organization. Maybe something good came out of it, maybe not, but move forward either way. Your emotions influence how others react, so move on so everyone else will too."

This is truly the scary part, since wallowing in the failure can become comfortable over time. The most important thing is to survive the cycles of business success and failure. Don't fall too deep when you fail, and don't fly too high when you succeed. There is nothing wrong with wallowing in the failure or celebrating the success for a week or so, but then regain the humility and be ready to ride the next cycle.

A Chinese proverb says "Falling hurts least [for] those who fly low." Even when you are flying (quite an amazing feat in itself) and things are going well in business, fly low with humility and common sense.

Collin Anderson achieves this by playing a game with himself all the time: "I try not to let the highs get too high or the lows too low. You won't make it if you do. I've worked to keep my emotions in a middle ground, but there's a downside to going too far. You can begin to lose the ability to feel joy or pain, and that's no way to go through life. When things are going badly, I tell myself that it's always darkest just before the dawn."

Letting Go of the Embrace

There is a great Buddhist parable that shows the true challenge of letting go of what has happened in the past. Two monks are walking by a river on their way back to the monastery. They hear a woman in a bride's dress crying by the river. The monks find out that she needs to cross the river to get to her wedding, but she us afraid she will ruin her bridal dress.

This particular sect of monks was prohibited from touching women in any way, but one of the monks ignores this precept, picks up the woman, and carries her across the river, thus saving her gown. The second monk is angry and scolds the first monk. This tirade lasts the entire way back to the monastery. But the first monk's mind is focused on the sunshine and listening to nature around him.

After returning to the monastery, he goes to bed. In the middle of the night, the second monk wakes him and says, "How could you carry that woman across the stream? You know it is forbidden."

"What woman?" the first monk asks.

The second monk says, "Don't you remember? The woman you carried across the river!"

"Of course," replies the first monk. "I only carried her across the stream, but you have carried her all the way back to the monastery!"

Shame is the glue that keeps us stuck in the past. Letting go is absolutely necessary to develop crazy business confidence.

Jon Sapir has had a very successful career in technology. But over the past few years he has invested his life savings in his new company and has never made a profit. As he reflects on what has happened, he sees the most important part is that "you've got to let go of the past. It's the first step and it's hard. You don't like to accept the failure, but you have to. Once you've accepted it, there has to be a period of looking around and really trying to understand what you learned and then how you can apply those lessons and move forward, and that's the stage that I'm at right now. It's just like any relationship except this one is with *failure*."

Written All over Your Face

When I was growing up and did something bad, my mother told me that what I had done was written all over my face. Too bad it's not the same way in business. Imagine if we could look at a businessperson and instantly know where he had been and what he had experienced.

When I was in New Zealand in 2006, I visited many attractions that featured the Maoris (pronounced "maah-ri"), the natives of the "Land of the White Cloud." Since their culture does not have a written language, these people paint tattoos on their faces to tell the history of their lives. These are not shame marks since they are actually reserved for the noble among the tribes.

These facial tattoos tell about their ancestors, their children, and their profession. They recount the wars that have been fought and the children who have been born. When Maoris die, their children carve the faces and tattoos of the deceased into wood so they are preserved forever.

What if, as businesspeople, we tattooed our experiences, both good and bad, on our faces? We could recount when we had masterful wins and dismal failures. We could list the prestigious positions we've held and the ones we lost. We could show where we made a lot of money and where we went broke. We could show those we helped and those we hurt. With inscribed faces, we would be unable to hide our failures and be forced to acknowledge all that we had experienced. Imagine how much easier it would make introductions!

CHAPTER 8

Failure Provides Choices

At my wedding, my best man, Zane stood up to give the toast and recounted the story of our bachelor party in Las Vegas a few weeks earlier. He told of my frustration at the blackjack table where I was really upset that I was losing my money. He reminded me that my luck would change soon.

"Lady Luck will soon shine on you again," he encouraged me at the casino. I retorted that what bothered me wasn't watching my chips getting whittled down; it was that in not winning, I was a loser.

At that point in my life, I hated to lose. I had read so many motivational books that I desperately wanted to remain a winner and be honored as such, the way I had been at IBM, so I went to great lengths to avoid losing. This pattern kept me working at IBM far past the time that I was satisfied with what I was doing there. Other people were called losers, but not I. I was one of the winners, and I was going to stay one of the winners . . . until I failed miserably.

Why play unless we think we can win? My father-in-law always played the state lottery because, as he so often said, "Someone has to win; it might as well be me," and he did win small stakes on occasion.

Now I'm not suggesting that you head to the nearest casino boat and buy some chips, but we can learn a lot from Las Vegas and lottery analogies.

Whether you play the lottery or not, you don't have to be a gambler to fail. No matter what you do (and don't do) in business, eventually failure will show up. It might be big, it might be small, but failure will arrive. Over the years, I've learned to regard it as no big deal. (All right, maybe not exactly *no* big deal, but certainly much less of a big deal.)

You and I are not the first people in business to fail. We have lots of company—and we're likely to have more. If this book teaches only one thing, it is how to learn to recognize, accept, and embrace failure as part of the natural sequence of events. This is how we already think of success; can we think of failure this way, too, as simply a natural outcome?

In business, certain odds are against us from the start. Since 80 percent of all new businesses fail within five years, you might as well learn to handle it. In fact, if you can start building this mind-set before you fail the first time, you'll be ahead of the game.

After I had gone out of business twice, the possibility of that happening a third time seemed easy to handle. If that doesn't sound quite so crazy as it might have when you picked up this book, that's a sign that you are making progress toward developing your own brand of resiliency and true business confidence before you have multiple failure notches on your belt.

If Las Vegas gambling is hard to relate to, consider the "Competitor's Creed" that is popular among the Fellowship of Christian Athletes.

I give my all—all of the time.

I do not give up.

I do not give in.

I do not give out. I am the Lord's warrior—

a competitor by conviction

and a disciple of determination.[1]

It is good to be a competitor and not want to lose. An honest competitor gives every deal his all, is rigorous about preparation and training, and approaches each event with humility and without the fear of losing.

I want to win. I expect to win. I celebrate when I win. But I can also accept when I lose. I learn what I can. I may wallow in it for a while, but then I move on. I escape to a new path. I try again. I view the outcome as an escape so I can now make a new choice. This is how my bounce acts.

Lost? Try the Escape Hatch

Anna Belyaev of Type A, a training firm in Chicago, knows that she will fail at parts of her business, but her resiliency makes it into a game where she really can't lose. "The game I play around failure is that I try to make sure that when I leap or take a risk, it's a big enough one that if I fall, I am just going to be so far ahead from where I started that it's not failure."

Belyaev works at her life so that any potential failures are ones that she knows can move her forward. In this way, with very long leaps, she can see any failure as progress on the path toward her goal, and even if she doesn't achieve what she wanted to achieve at a particular step, at the very least she lands a long way from where she started. From this new place, she then has a different view to make a decision that will yield the best possible outcome.

Deborah House knows that people are sad and disappointed when they fail, but she retorts that we need to "see how quickly you can come out of it. I view it as a process of elimination because even the best of plans have the option for failure, so by failing you've eliminated one of your options and you have a smaller pool to choose from."

Failure thus can be viewed as an escape hatch for each step. Finding out what doesn't work is as important as finding out what does—and there is no doubt that failure teaches us what doesn't work. When we fail, we have eliminated at least one of the possibilities.

Failure actually can be very cleansing. It gives us the ability to start anew with a modified or entirely new direction or outlook that has a new opportunity (and probability) for success. The moment we jettison what happened, we have a fresh chance to succeed (or to fail). We can get moving once again and begin a new streak.

Mary Schmich, a columnist and master storyteller for the *Chicago Tribune,* sums up losing this way: "Sometimes losing is like a soft rain at the end of a searing desert day. It comes as a relief. Losing can be liberation, reorientation, freeing you to do something gentler on your soul. And at the very least, losing always makes a pretty good story."[2]

Getting to No

I'm perpetually a salesperson at heart, and this has always served me well. When my businesses fail, one of the things I always tell myself is that if things get really bad, I can go back into sales. Even when economic times are really bad, a good salesperson (and many who are not so good) can always find a job.

Why is that? I think it's because not that many people go into sales and fewer still are successful at it. In sales you face what looks like (and often feels like) failure every single day, sometimes several times a day. Most people don't enjoy and, therefore, don't seek out that kind of constant pressure. My father hated sales. While we were growing up, he told us to take any job except one in sales. That's probably why both my brother and I eventually did end up in sales!

But this aspect of sales—the repeated failure—perhaps more than any other, really prepares you to handle the rest of the process of business and life with reconstituted resiliency. It was through sales (although I didn't recognize it at the time) that I built the foundation of bounce. For those of us who can take it, the daily cycle of yes and no will fast-forward us on our way to build a solid, confident foundation, since we will take the answers our prospects give us in stride.

When making sales call, I believe that to get to yes, I have to first get to no with the prospect to find out whether they represent a real opportunity. This may seem counterintuitive since we all know we can't close an order without a yes. But a no is useful. It tells me that the prospect is not in enough pain or doesn't see enough benefit in my offering to purchase it now. They are a false prospect. A no is much better than an unreturned phone call, or a maybe, or a "Gee, I'm just not sure." I know how to work with a no. I understand no.

In the sales process, most of us don't lose to a competitor; rather we lose to "no decision" or to "no response"—in other words, not hearing back from the prospect. Recognize that the absence of a decision is really a no and that, as hard as it is to let go of what we thought was an excellent prospect who praised us and told us on our sales call what we wanted to hear, we must accept that they will not be buying from us yet. Here is another place where we can learn from the Buddhist monk who let go after he had carried the bride across the river.

Hesh Reinfeld, a humorist, realized the value of a no when he was chasing the opportunity to be a business-humor commentator on National Public Radio (NPR). The NPR editor loved what Reinfeld had to offer and recorded his initial commentary. Reinfeld then waited for it to air—and waited, and waited, and waited. He later found out that the executive producer (the editor's boss) did not find the piece at all funny and killed it. Still, Reinfeld did not give up. He kept talking to the editor, and she kept saying how much she liked his humor, but nothing ever happened.

Finally Hesh called and said, "'Just tell me it won't work and I'll stop bothering you every week.' She said, 'Hesh, I feel so bad, I really like your humor but my boss doesn't.' I said. 'You can say no, it's okay, I'm a big boy.' She finally said it, 'No.' I never called again. I still wonder what would have happened had I gotten on national radio."[3]

A big part of learning how to spring back is knowing when to stop pursuing an opportunity. That's why, as Hesh learned, a no from a prospect can be almost as good as a yes.

When a salesperson gets a no, does this mean that he failed? Not to me, it doesn't. As for Hesh, he learned to stop wondering about a missed opportunity. He writes that it's "like meeting your high school sweetheart who dumped you senior year. You see her every Christmas and you know what? She still looks good, maybe even a little hot. But remember you haven't done so poorly yourself. It's what every religious tradition preaches, be happy with your lot."[4] I think it makes sense in business, too.

The good news is that once we hear (and I mean really *hear*) no, we will waste no more time on a path that does not have a real opportunity for success, at least not now. Most businesspeople spend too much time going down paths that will never produce success-ful outcomes. We want to change what doesn't want to happen into something that still can occur.

As one of the more tenacious people around, the *last* piece of advice (free or for fee) that I would ever offer a reader or one of my clients is that they should give up easily. However, if the signs are there (a nondecision, five unreturned phone calls, or a hard no) then we cannot afford to ignore that information.

If we were driving on a highway and the signs said the highway was ending, wouldn't we stop? We need to realize as a hungry sales rat that the cheese we thought was in that hole isn't there. Too often we keep burrowing down that hole, hoping to smell more cheese, when there was never any cheese in the first place.

Pursuing failure can become very comfortable since we at least know how to get to the rat hole, how to burrow, and how to sniff for cheese. Unfortunately, empty rat hole scenarios provide little oppor-tunity for success.

Realize that the cheese is gone or wasn't there in the first place. Accept the failure as fact. In economic terms, "What's sunk is sunk."[5]

Stop piling more bad decisions and choices on top of the ones you already made. Have the bounce to change your path so you can search for a new hole where there might be some cheese.

The fifth building band is to understand that *failure gives you choices*. A no gives you an escape to pursue a path that has a fresh opportunity for success.

My Least Favorite Teacher

Veteran writer Jeff Wuorio tells us that "if business success is a set of *Cliff Notes*, business failure is a lifelong mentor."[6] Calling it a lifelong tormentor would probably be more accurate. Tracy Thirion, founder of Bamboo Worldwide, goes so far as to say that part of being in business is being a martyr: "You have to struggle for it."

Without the bumps and scars, we don't learn what we don't know. Without them, we don't pay enough attention to the roadblocks or the pitfalls to learn from our challenges. In a *Forbes* magazine report, The Limited founder Les Wexner (his company bought Roy Raymond's Victoria's Secret) states that we need to "make mistakes faster. If you're not pushing hard enough to make big blunders, you're not playing the game at the appropriate pace." "Fail forward fast" is his motto.

The fashion industry in Europe is no stranger to failure. Alberto Alessi, Italian product designer, believes that you need to actually revel in failure. "Dance on the borderline between success and disaster. Because that's where your next big breakthrough will come from."[7] It is reported that Alessi even takes more pride than most in his flops. He puts all his failed products in a private museum where he has weekly discussions with his designers. He published a book of prototypes that never went into production. Alessi believes his failures remind him not to play it safe.

Richard Sheridan, who appeared on the cover of *Forbes* magazine in 2003, believes in experimenting often. "My mantra is to make mistakes faster, because a bunch of little mistakes along the way is easier to correct, and allows you to learn and adjust, much like when you learn to drive."

Dynamic Learners

But how do we learn to be better and make better choices? Not necessarily by practicing the same thing over and over again, especially if we are practicing wrong. As the business adage says, "If you keep doing what you have always done, you will get what you have always gotten." This is also one definition of insanity—doing the same thing over and over again and expecting different results. Like rooting around in the same mouse hole, looking for the same cheese that isn't there, doing things the same way (even if you aren't succeeding) can actually give you false confidence.

A client of mine, Matthew Daniels of the Dabaton Corporation[8], has being building a business for the past two years. He calls on Fortune 500 clients to sell his brand of marketing services. He is able to get appointments with top executives. They tell him they love his presentation and what he offers—but no one ever buys. Matthew suspects (and I know) that he must be doing something wrong—over and over again.

We grow in business through trial and error and through our own willingness to make mistakes, change our approach, and then make different mistakes. A key to business success is having many small failures and no fatal mistakes. Think of these small failures as a way to let a tiny bit of gas out of this can of soda pop called business so it does not explode.

In small doses, failure may be able to teach us something without killing us. Sometimes this is all we need—just the chance to capture enough from the last failure to give us a different look at the process so we can change things enough to have a shot (no matter how small) at a different outcome. But if, like my client Matthew, we don't change the way we are doing things, failure can't teach us anything but how to endure pain.

While visiting Melbourne, Australia, in 2006, I heard Professor Allan Gibb from the University of Durham in England remark that entrepreneurs are "dynamic learners" with an "experimentally based heuristic" for learning. That is certainly true for me. Most times, it seems that the only way I really learn something is to go out and try it every which way until I get it right. I am a naturally fast learner, and in my experience that's the case with most successful entrepreneurs.

Ian Patrick Sobieski, the managing director of the Band of Angels in Menlo Park, California, believes that to be successful at leading big groups requires applying a dynamic and broad set of rules, because the best decisions actually come from organizations or people that are not rule-bound. These decisions "can account at a human level for the complexities often involved, and tend to be quicker and more adaptable than rigid rules allow. This is an advantage of start-ups over large companies—their ability to act quickly, and to approach decisions with greater granularity than big groups." Whether they succeed or fail, they can react to the market.

Regardless of the success or failure of a specific event, people involved in start-up companies learn fast. This can be a brutal way to do business but it does build stamina, something that bounce feeds on. Many businesspeople and entrepreneurs whom I've met and worked with are unconsciously competent in this way. When I interviewed some of them for this book, most could cite chapter and verse on why they had failed at certain times, but more than a few really had no idea of exactly why they succeeded when they did.

Is there any truth to the idea that we can we learn something from failure? Perhaps. It is always good to go back and see if it can teach us anything. Certainly, there is not much to lose by briefly examining what and why it happened. When I was kicked out of my second business by my two partners, I learned how important people, specifically the partners we choose, are to a successful business.

However, grading our failures is useless and does not contribute to learning. A more useful approach is to view failure as something that just happens as part of the natural process, without characterizing it as good or bad.

Morphing into Your Next Success

We need to remain flexible and willing to change. At each new out-come (good or bad), we need to listen to the market and evolve our products or services depending on what the market wants or needs.

Plenty of businesses started out doing one thing and ended up being successful at something else.

- *eBay.* Started in 1995 as AuctionWeb, selling auction software. When the auctions proved profitable, they decided to sell Pez instead of software. After going public in 1998, eBay is now a $6 billion company.

- *Ball Corporation.* Started in 1880 by the Ball Brothers in Muncie, Indiana, to sell canning jars. This $6 billion company today is primarily into aerospace technology.

- *Nokia.* This $13 billion company, which started in 1865 selling rubber tires and boots, is now a renowned telecom-munications firm and sells mobile cellular phone devices worldwide.

- *COLECO.* The company's name is an acronym that stands for the COnnecticut LEather Company, founded in 1932. Much later on, they sold the toy Cabbage Patch Dolls.

- *Sprint.* This company started out as the Southern Pacific Railroad International in 1899. Now Sprint is a $10 billion force in the U.S. mobile telecommunications industry.

Kara Trott suggests that to know when you should morph, you must listen to your clients while you simultaneously follow your competitors. "Entrepreneurs are good at observation—at observing what people want, and then crafting their idea around that. Awareness and observation are what help you learn." This is why one of the important skills for gaining bounce and being resilient is to hone your observation skills and look for these building bands I am describing.

The one who wins isn't always the one who always perseveres. Perseverance and resiliency are not interchangeable. Evan Schwartz writes in Harvard Business School's *Working Knowledge* that "Perseverance must be accompanied by the embrace of failure. Failure is what moves you forward. Listen to failure."[9]

What are we listening for? Three things: everything, anything, and nothing. Stop looking and just listen to that new starting point. Listen to the sound of being unburdened from the past set of constraints. Listen to the cry of being born again. Listen to the rise of the sun on a new morning. Recognize it is your next chance for a totally different outcome.

Larry Terkel, a yoga teacher, business speaker, and author, professes that we need to seek ease when we find ourselves in the uncomfortable positions of life. When he teaches yoga, part of the process is for students to put themselves into formal positions or postures called *asanas*. For many of his students, these postures are difficult or painful to achieve. Larry emphasizes that they are "uncomfortable positions we put ourselves in so we find the ease in it." He tells his students that they have not mastered a yoga asana or posture until they can smile through the entire process. Therefore, he teaches that they are not "easy poses" but "poses with ease." He believes that we need to be ready to do them, commit to doing them, make any small adjustments to stay in them, and then enjoy them.

Similarly, we find ourselves in many difficult positions in business and may have a difficult time being in them with ease. Failure is one of these difficult positions. Like asanas, we need to find a way to hold failure with ease.

Start from Where You Are, Right Now

Business cycles (whether successful or not) drop us in different places throughout our lives. We can only make new decisions from where we are right now, not where we were three months ago before our last decision was made or where we hope to be three months out.

As much as we want to, we can't blink forward or go back. If you want to develop true business confidence, stop thinking that your business should be in a different place than where you are. Stop telling yourself that you should not be here. Stop playing the "if only" game. Stop thinking that the way things are is not fair or is someone else's fault. Instead, think about what you can do next to get the best possible outcome from the place you are right now.

Never stay in one place longer than you need to. Look around and observe where you are, plot your next move, and then make it. I am not necessarily in favor of "ready, fire, aim," but I do think that in business we spend far too much time planning what we are going to do, rather than simply doing it. Talking about the decision that needs to be made and considering it is many times a good thing, but somewhere along the line you have to act.

In karate, teachers are constantly counseling the class to "be quiet and just watch the moves and do them." I need to get out of my head and into my body through action and just learn it by doing. This is similar to what Malcolm Gladwell said in his book *Blink* (Little, Brown and Company, 2005): Believing that talk, discussion, and rationalization always find the best outcome is just nonsense. Instead, Gladwell calls for snap judgments.

Like Gladwell, I believe that we make our best decisions in an instant. The rest of the time is spent justifying our course of action and our decision-making process. No matter what, some action is always better than no action at all. This doesn't mean that we immediately run off in a different direction without thinking. It does mean that unless we deliberately *do something* we are deliberately *doing nothing*. There is no in-between.

Patient Passion—Choose Intensity

As businesspeople, it is imperative that we be intense. The heat from burning brightly will keep us going on those cold days that can seem never-ending. When we engage in our chosen business activity to its fullest extent, business intensity can close the distance between short-term failure and long-term success. Winston Churchill defined success as "going from failure to failure without a loss of enthusiasm."

In the summer of 2006, Brett Farmiloe, Daniel Weber, and Tamir Greenberg traveled around the United States in a large recreational vehicle on what they called the "Pursue the Passion Tour,"[10] interviewing over 100 people about their passion. They asked the simple question of how people gain confidence. Whenever they asked this of people who have successfully made a career out of a personal passion, the answer they received sounded like a broken record, because every respondent said, "Practice!" In their three months of travel and interviewing, what they learned is that through practicing, you acquire the confidence needed to achieve dreams and travel beyond your goals.

Brett recounts:

> Passion offsets the fear that cripples confidence, because when you are pursuing something with a passion, the excitement that radiates off that inner drive will far outweigh the fear of failing. Passion will make you rise in the early hours and make you retire late into the night, but it doesn't matter because time is not a factor when you are doing something you love. It will lead you to persevere when you don't feel like practicing, and will rekindle the fire when other factors attempt to extinguish the

flames. But when passion is nonexistent, the desire to practice will start to fade, and the confidence that was once being carefully constructed will become stagnant and slowly start to disappear.

Intensity thwarts best efforts, producing the end results that build confidence. By approaching practice with intensity, you will be able to test your talent and strive to reach your potential. Intense practices result in continuous improvements upon previous achievements, and it is through these personal accomplishments that confidence is crafted. Without an intense approach these small successes and triumphs never take place, and the positive reinforcement that goes along with these personal victories diminishes.

Passion is an everyday, maybe every minute, thing. After a lot of initial success, Brian Gallagher, formerly the CFO at Preon, a power utility service company, struggled with turning his financially ailing company around for years. Through it all, he never lost his weekly intensity or optimism. Brian recounts his experience of coming into the office after the weekend: "Every Monday, I come to the office thinking this is the week that will turn us around. I think I'm fortunate that I sincerely believe that every Monday. I know that this Monday won't be any different." He was forced to resign from the company before he was able to affect a full turnaround.

Larry Cunningham talks about difficult days and how he is still unwilling to give up his dream. "I have been scared as hell but I absolutely love what I'm doing. Thinking about another job just ticks me off. Early on, I hadn't been bloodied yet. Talk about humility—what a humbling experience this has been." Larry spends most of his days alone in his office contacting interested prospects from trade shows and other vendor activities.

Colin Jones maintains his energy by being excited that he will achieve something. "I think entrepreneurs have a natural ability to see the big picture and hold that out in front of them and it holds this energy, this attraction to this goal, and releases energy back to you and surrounding whatever it is that you're doing. I think a true entrepreneur can readjust their goal at the drop of a hat, say, okay, that's going to happen today, that's for the future, and then move their goal, just readjust things without a lot of emotional failure."

Developing business confidence and resiliency is about holding on to that passion. Absorbing multiple failures and letting go of our passionate vision yields only stoic cynicism. We will only remember the bad stuff, and holding on to it will poison any chance for success. If we feel like losers, we might become losers. If we think we will never succeed again, we probably won't.

Gail Blanke believes success is all about using passion to see yourself and your business from different viewpoints. "Passion drives profits, whether you're running a business of your own or you're in a corporation. The best people inside corporations have an entrepreneurial spirit; they're always looking for the new thing, a new way of doing it, a new way of seeing themselves."[11]

Passion creates the opportunity to fight through the failure if that is necessary. Collin Anderson says, "When you're an entrepreneur, if you don't fight through it, no one else will. If you don't come to work, there's nobody else working on it. There's no free ride. Everything is going to be like it was the day before unless you do what needs to be done. When we had big problems, I didn't sleep. I would wake up with an idea, try it, and then it failed. And then something would break in a positive way. A lot of it is hanging in there and fighting through it. My sense is that people are more capable than they think. I got into it, and realized that I was okay."

Family-run businesses grow faster, and one of the reasons they do may be their passion. In 2003, *Business Week* stated that the annual profit growth at S&P 500 family-run businesses over the past 10 years is 21.1 percent, while nonfamily companies grew at 12.6 percent. "In part, it's having managers with passion for the enterprise that goes far beyond that of any hired executives, no matter how much they are paid."[12]

The most important thing for anyone seeking true confidence is to retain passion, humility, and vision. Keep asking, why am I here?

Why am I doing whatever I am doing today? Where do I think I am going? Tap into personal energy. Businesspeople who survive the cycles of success and failure while retaining their passion keep trying different approaches and do eventually succeed again. Passion facilitates the choice, which in turns feeds the passion and keeps the business cycle going.

Passion, Confidence, and the Bottomless Bounce

Over the long run, passion is the only thing that will bounce the businessperson off the bottom. Choice feeds the passion, and passion drives the bounce. Trying to keep your drive up by chasing the brass ring (read "financial gain") during challenging times can't provide the necessary motivation for a person to keep going.

We need to understand where our passion comes from. Mine comes from two sources: the desire to provide for my family, and the need to see my ideas succeed or fail to make a difference in the world. Passion yields sustenance when it is needed most. On those cold days of failure, the only thing that sustains us is our passion.

It never becomes easy to fail—and we don't want it to—but Nicholas Hall says that it becomes easier to bounce back. "That's the really important thing—to get back up at the plate and to start to understand over time it's just part of the process. And that you have to stay in the game. You don't have more time. You've got right now. The next second is a crap shoot."[13]

The way to build true business confidence is by actually being in the middle of the business mess with your passion and realizing that no matter what happens, it isn't going to render you dead. As Anna Belyaev says, "By taking risks, by discovering that very little kills you, by surviving, you can do a lot more than you thought; staying in conversation and healthy competition with others, so you can have a sense of where you are in the pack."

Passion will actually renew the physical body we require; it will also renew the emotional spirit that we crave. There is no substitute. Family support and excellent employees are critical to success, but either of these may not be there when we fail. At those times, passion sustains, absolutely. It is our internal strength when the other supports don't hold.

CHAPTER 9

Do It Anyway: Be a Smart Risk Taker

To have the opportunity to win, you have to be able to stay in the game. Play to win, but only play if you can absorb the loss. If you bet too much and then make a fatal mistake that bankrupts your business, you are out of the game with no opportunity to succeed.

This isn't to say that you can't take risks that don't pay off. You must take risks, and some of them will fail. However, often small mistakes can do the job of larger ones, allowing you the opportunity (*opportunity,* not *guarantee*) to incrementally make your way to success. This is where humility comes in to calibrate the showmanship. Unfortunately, when ego is driving, only a large mistake will inspire a change of approach.

Rick Mazurksy, an experienced executive in the toy industry, recounts when his company entered the road-racing business and obtained the license to market Indy 500 winner Johnny Ruthersford:

> We hired him as spokesperson to endorse our product. He invited us down to the Indy time trials, and we invited our clients and salespeople. We got to get up close, go into the pits; it was an exciting day. During the time trials prior to dinner, Rutherford's engine blew, but he came to

dinner nonetheless. While we were enjoying cocktails, he had ice water. We thought he would be really down. "What are you going to do?" I asked him. "I'm going to get myself another car," he said. "There are 33 starting positions. All I have to do is get in the race. If you get into the race, you will always have a chance to win."

Johnny Ruthersford knew what he had to do to stay in the game, and, as a well-connected and wealthy Indy racer, he had enough reserves to carry it off.

Many start-up entrepreneurs risk too much of their own or family capital; their potential return—*if* they achieve it, which most do not—is not worth the odds they accept. They are blinded by their passion. However, if we recognize that statistically entrepreneurs have an 80 percent chance of failing and we can survive the likely consequences of those kinds of odds, then it is our risk to take.

Sometimes people can't be passionate or resilient when they fail because the stakes are simply too high. That's why I always tell aspiring entrepreneurs that if they have too much to lose, maybe they should reconsider playing in the start-up game. This is an important point to examine closely and internalize. It is glamorous in our culture to play for all the marbles. Talk about crazy: Once I played a racquetball match for the title to my car. I lost the car.[1] This is not the kind of crazy you want to be.

We love the bravado of those who put it all on the line—put your money on black and let the roulette wheel spin. "Let it ride" is a too familiar rallying cry. This is just plain stupid. Bragging rights only last until the wheel stops spinning or you win. The casino actually has about 5 percent advantage at the roulette table—and that 5 percent margin is one of the most disadvantageous to the gambler anywhere on the floor.

Everyone who starts a business is a risk taker. I always joke that if entrepreneurs knew the risk they were taking, there is no way they would start. However, we can make better decisions with improved outcomes if we can learn to be better risk takers. We need to learn from our increased awareness and observation, silencing our ego in the process for this to work.

But the risks that we take aren't actually one huge risk; we can be more effective decision makers by breaking down those huge, risky choices into smaller steps. This can improve our overall odds of success by inviting more but smaller failures, affording us more choices for midcourse corrections and ultimately more opportunities for success. Here are some of the risks we need to consider:

- *Financial.* Everyone focuses on this since it is the easiest to identify. It's the money. Bet wrong or too big and you can lose everything—your savings, your house, your car, or your job.

- *Opportunity.* When you choose to do a thing, you are also choosing *not* to do something else. There is an opportunity risk in everything we do. Consider what has been gained or lost as a result of choosing or not choosing.

- *Health.* The stress that risk produces can literally kill us. When I was diagnosed with diabetes in 1995 at the age of 35, the doctors told me the stress of running my businesses had caused a virus that brought on the disease. When we used to vacation at an exclusive beach in South Haven, Michigan, I met many men walking along the beach with their shirts off and their open heart surgery scars still showing purple in the sun. Work literally can kill you.

- *Family.* Many business decisions result in a lot of stress on the family. Business is particularly difficult on the spouse or partner who many times has no idea what is going on (because we don't tell them). Failed business adventures many times result in poor parenting and failed marriages.

- *Reputation.* A failed business, especially in cultures and countries outside the United States, can destroy reputations and eliminate any other opportunity to succeed. Money is easier to recover than reputation.

Understanding how to *make smarter decisions* when it comes to risk and thus *become a better risk taker* is the sixth building band for gaining true business confidence. This is achieved by establishing a preferred process and outcome for every choice and then asking some key questions, as follows.

What Exactly Is It Going to Take to Reach My Preferred Outcome?

We can all set lofty goals, but many of us have no game plan to reach our objectives. We love to make large proclamations since that is often what society asks us to do. Because there is a mountain out there, we must climb it. Big deal!

Many small businesses want to be major players without having a clear idea of how much bigger to grow and how to get there. I read a lot of business plans from aspiring entrepreneurs about how they will be a $50 million business in five years, but often there is no capital or marketing plan to support those goals.

Goals must be built from the ground up, like a series of stairs. What early steps get us to a particular goal? What are the interim goals that need to be achieved? What are the critical success factors to those? Are one or more factors common to multiple goals? Which will be tackled first? What will be the basis for setting priorities?

When I took up karate five years ago, I knew I wanted to earn a black belt, but before I could get there, I needed to go through the eight color belt ranks. I had to whittle back my aim.

Far-off goals are fine to set since they add vision, but setting smaller, intermediate goals and realizing those small successes or readjusting from smaller, interim failures will actually put you in a better decision-making position to reach the larger goals you set.

What Are the Possible Failures That I May Encounter?

Have we mapped out where our best chance of failure will come from? In the traditional business SWAT (strengths, weaknesses, advantages, and threats) analysis, failure falls into the weaknesses and threats part of the equation.

However, too often failure comes from some very unlikely sources. When your business is doing this analysis, ask, where are we most likely to be surprised by failure? That's a good first place to look. If any of the failures you can anticipate should come to pass, what will your response be? What is your contingency plan? How can you capitalize on your strengths and advantages when your business has been damaged by your weaknesses?

You can extend the effectiveness of the standard SWAT analysis not by figuring out all that can go wrong, but by preparing for failures that may come, especially the ones that appear by surprise. Minimizing the potential effects of these less-than-desirable outcomes gives us another chance at success. We get to stay in the game.

For This Goal, What Are the Possible Rewards?

Too few entrepreneurs ask this important question: When I strive for a particular goal, what will my actual rewards be? How will I measure them, and in what time frame can I reasonably expect to achieve them? Will I be satisfied with the reward when I attain it?

I have encountered many businesspeople who, when they achieve their goal, ask, "Is this all?" This is especially true if their only goal is money. Money almost never succeeds as the sole source of satisfaction. Consider the many lottery winners who are still unhappy after achieving the financial windfall.[2] This surprises us because many of us believe that money equals happiness. Nearly one-third of lottery winners eventually become bankrupt.[3]

Evelyn Adams won the New Jersey lottery twice, scoring more than $5 million. Ms. Adams now lives in a trailer—and not on the Malfi Coast—partly because so many people wanted her money, she never learned to say no, and also because she continued to gamble and lost much of the money playing slot machines.

William Post won $16.2 million in the Pennsylvania lottery and now survives on Social Security and food stamps. His brother was arrested for hiring a hit man to kill Post—the brother hoped to inherit some of the money. A former girlfriend sued Post for some of the cash, and other siblings pestered him to invest in business ventures that failed. Post also spent time in jail for firing a gun over a bill collector's head. A year after winning the lottery, he was $1 million in debt.

Suzanne Mullins won $4.2 million in the Virginia State lottery. After lending money to a company, using her winnings as collateral on a loan, and lending her uninsured son-in-law $1 million to deal with an illness, she is deeply in debt. She borrowed money that she agreed to pay back with her yearly checks. Then the lottery changed the rules so that winners could collect the winnings as a lump sum. Mullins took the one-time payment but didn't pay back the loan.

Financial gain is always the most easily stated goal, but stop to consider what other rewards you could gain from undertaking a given risk, besides money. Most entrepreneurs do not build companies merely to make money; they build them because they have a passion to see their ideas succeed. They want to create something from nothing.

The day after I sold my last business, my partner and I participated in an all-night bicycle ride that happens in Chicago once a year. On that ride, we talked about our years building the company together. Of course we were glad that we had sold the business for a financial profit, but more importantly, we had created something of value for our clients and employees where there had been nothing before. As stated before, this had always been one of my driving sources of passion.

It is a common practice for business owners to frame the first dollar that they earn. (I never got the chance to frame the first dollar from any of our businesses, since the transactions were not done in cash.) It isn't the dollar itself, but rather what the dollar represents. Every business owner is proud of and remembers the moment that the first customer actually bought a product or service from them.

So ask yourself, what are the possible meaningful rewards besides money? Those rewards are passion fuel. I am a motivational speaker not only because I can make money at it. The two most important rewards for me are (1) through my message, I get an opportunity to make a difference in another businessperson's life; and (2) when I speak, I experience the deep enjoyment of being totally in that moment as the energy flows out from me and back in from my audience.

The best part is that these results, unlike others in business, are immediate. When I finish a story I can tell right away what impact it has had on my audience. I can tell after a speech, when they relay their personal stories to me, that I made a difference in their business life that day.

Is the Reward I Might Obtain Worth the Risk?

The financial return for most entrepreneurs does not equal the financial and emotional risk that they take in starting a business. But, as already discussed, entrepreneurs don't take these risks only for the money. As businesspeople, we need to examine the other end of the equation: Given what we know about the risks and rewards, if we reach our goal, will it have been worth it in addition to or instead of the money?

The sides of this question don't necessarily need to balance like a mathematical equation, but you need to reach an answer that is satisfactory to you. Don't settle for an "of course" or a quick yes. The good risk taker has an honest answer before he starts a venture. Many times after I have examined this part of the equation I found that the answer for me was no—the reward was not worth the risks. But sometimes—more often in my earlier business years than now— I found myself trying to achieve the goal anyway because I followed my own blind ambition (read "ego").

When is the reward not worth the risk? This is the case when you are unable to survive a loss or failure—when you are betting so much of your resources (money, energy, reputation, or whatever) on one shot that if you miss it this one time you are out of the game.

The reward is also not worth the risk when you gain a reward that really does not get you any closer to your ultimate goal. You may be trying to achieve something only out of greed, revenge, or some other negative motive. This is not very smart, but you can find yourself involved in this form of inertia, especially where money is involved.

Many conquering armies have forged ahead to attack a new country simply because it was there and they were there, and it seemed to be the next logical thing to do. What if the Germans had considered the risks of attacking Russia in the wintertime instead of only focusing on the possible reward? There may have been a different outcome to World War II.

How Well Do I Know Myself?

When I make the decision to take the risk to achieve the reward, if I fail, can I handle it financially and emotionally? One way to predict this is to see how you have reacted in the past when things don't go your way. The most recent experience can be a good predictor of how you will react the next time in a similar situation.

If you fall apart at the first sign of failure, you may not be suited to taking much risk. When you lose money, are you able to recover or do you simply spiral down? Are you able to reach out to your family and friends if you need to? Will they be supportive if you do? Many friends and family members become so afraid for you that they can actually scare you into feeling worse. They sometimes become the bad Samaritan, not wanting to deal with failure and taking a bit of joy in saying "I told you so" as they watch you fail.

The way that Anna Belyaev tries to pull out of the emotional fear of business risks is to reinvent it as a game: "You know, like when you're a kid, you play baseball and recruit other kids to play your game;

you won or lost, had a great time. But that's not how we play adult life. Our businesses, everything becomes really important. If I reinvent it as a game, then I say what kind of game am I playing, what positions are being filled? Then I invite people to play it and it becomes fun."

In this way, Anna considers the entire game and the end result she wants before she starts. She does this by focusing on the whole process instead of considering only the outcome.

Who Here Can Help?

To be successful, one needs a good business support structure beyond family and friends. Many entrepreneurs wait to ask for help until they have two days of cash flow left, because to ask for help might mean admitting defeat. Realizing you need help before it is too late is the critical revelation—*asking* for it before it is too late is a sign of business confidence. Before we get to "What's sunk is sunk," what action can we take that might possibly improve our odds?

Good risk takers understand what they are good at and where they need help. For example, something I often see in start-up companies is the founding entrepreneur being unwilling to relinquish any control. But no growing business can operate with the CEO making every decision, no matter how knowledgeable that person is.

Reaching out and asking for help is the most difficult task facing any businessperson, whether they are in success or failure mode. Associate with smart people who want to contribute to your process. Entrepreneurs have to wear many hats, but no entrepreneur can successfully wear them all. When you don't know something, find someone who does. This is especially difficult for men in our self-reliant culture. Just think, many of us won't even ask for directions when we are lost!

Jeff King, CEO of PSD Consulting in Chicago, is constantly taking to other people and reading all he can. "I know when I read I learn a lot. I attend business functions—whether it's a seminar or a focus group. I've gone and listened to experienced businesspeople, and you learn from them how to get involved in a group like that and asked to speak, how did they research their topic, become so knowledgeable, how did they get the confidence to speak up there. Learn from other people in business so they can be a teacher; listen and learn from them."

For some people, asking for help is the same as admitting defeat. For example, I refuse to read the directions before assembling something. That would be too easy. When I can't figure it out and have to go back to the directions, I feel like a loser. In this way, I set myself up to fail.

In business I've learned the hard way that asking for help isn't losing. I've learned to think of it as adding to a winning team. A sports win happens because of a team effort, not just one person. Business is very much a team sport. But, as many people who have worked with me will tell you, this hasn't come easily or automatically to me, regardless of how important I know it is.

Gail Blanke observes that "In trapezing, every trapeze artist has a catcher. A catcher is the person who reaches out, takes your hands at exactly the right moment, not a minute too soon, nor a minute too late. A catcher understands you, and your rhythm and your vision. There's a saying in trapezing: Let the catcher do the catching."[4]

Blanke believes that you need to find those people whom you "trust, count on, and listen to. You have to have catchers, you have to have advisers, and you have to listen to them. When they say you've taken this thing far enough, let's change direction, because they care about you and they have perhaps a clearer perspective than you, then you have to listen." Blanke believes that being successful in business is about taking risk, but not "reckless risk," as she calls it. "There is a difference. It's probably a fine line, but your catchers can help you not go over that fine line."[5]

Am I Observing How Risk Changes?

How can we judge if the risk in a particular situation is increasing or lessening? I am asked by clients many times, "How can I know if I should continue running this business or give up and close it down?"

The first measure of risk is found in the cash flow statement and on the balance sheet. Is operating the business increasing my cash flow without reducing my assets, or is operating the business reducing my cash flow and depleting assets? If ongoing operations steadily deplete your cash, and you are unable to identify an event that will reverse its course, it is time to close up shop.

Your balance sheet will tell you how much cash and other assets you have to sustain any losses. A good ratio to look at is the *quick ratio* (also called the *acid test*) of current assets over current liabilities. This gives business owners a good idea of their ability to meet their current obligations. If this number gets to be less than 1, the risk to your business is substantial. The optimal number will vary by industry; make it your business to know what it is for the industry that you are in.

Risk also changes if your personal passion meter goes up or down. How much do you still enjoy coming to work every day? If your passion wanes, your risk of making poor decisions and not being able to survive spikes. If your passion becomes fanatical and you stop examining processes and outcomes, then your risk has also gone up—you have entered the very dangerous zealot phase. You are making decisions based only on ego and not based on the best business evaluation you can apply. You are no longer listening to the counsel of the people around you or being guided by humility. You are ignoring the signals the market is giving you. It makes you keep going when, for all economical and practical purposes, you should quit.

How can we judge whether we have been blinded by passion, or whether passion is only providing the fuel we need to keep us working toward the positive outcome we seek? This is very difficult to answer in a universal way. Focusing passion short-term on examining each process and outcome, and not becoming blindly ideological in our business beliefs, lets us test our passion against each successive outcome when it happens.

Listen to your closest advisers. See what the people you have trusted over the years are telling you. They can always, and I mean *always,* see things about your situation that you can't. They can't all be wrong if they have given good counsel in the past. Ask them if your passion is fueling your ego instead of fueling your business. Ask them if you have lost your humility.

Also watch the direction of the traffic. Are the good customers, employees, and vendors jumping off your business ship? Is it hard to remember the last time you spoke in a normal tone of voice? Do you keep telling yourself that they "just don't get it" or that they are "not a believer"?

If everyone is against you all at once, something is wrong—most likely with you or with the way you are looking at things. When this is happening, temper your passion by asking yourself why people are leaving; try to think the way they are thinking. Go to your most trusted adviser or pay an expert stranger to help you evaluate your risk. Take their advice about what you should do next.

Every time you lose a key employee, manager, or client, your risk increases. Losing key employees is probably the largest risk since it will takes time, energy, and money to replace someone who was a valuable part of your business. The risk involves the cost to fill the position as well as the lost revenue of the position being vacant or being filled temporarily by someone else with less training.

Be aware of how changing risk will affect the process and the outcome. As the risk changes, assess what the process will look like in the new situation and make a decision in the direction of the optimal outcome. Risk is part of any business and career. Accept it, but look more deeply at risk's many faces and how they change over time.

CHAPTER 10

A Little DAB will Do Ya![i] Drive, Accept, and Build

It's All about the Process, Dilbert

In the 1970s, there was a contest called the Kremer Prize for the first group that could build an airplane that would take off under solely human power and fly a mile before landing. Groups entered from many famed American technical institutions like MIT and Caltech. Ironically, the winner was a group of hobbyists led by Paul MacCready, whose team made up for their lack of theory with a design that allowed fast repair. Their airplane, the *Gossamer Albatross*, could be fixed quickly and inexpensively after they crashed it over and over again.

> Each of these experiments—you couldn't really call them accidents— was a highly context-sensitive tutorial in the trade-offs possible among strength, weight, and cost. When a part failed . . . that failure did much more than testify to an inadequacy in the original design: *the timing, severity, and path* of the failure underlined the issue needing attention next and pointed suggestively in the direction of a likely solution.[1]

When MacCready and his team failed, the failure pointed to the next issue that needed attention, and they then would make that change. The *Gossamer Albatross* crashed 500 times. An observer at the time quipped that if they had let the airplane crash 1,000 times it probably would have flown many more miles. You can guess the ending of this story: The *Gossamer Albatross* won the prize.

We can learn a lot from MacCready. Drive for what you want, and accept the result you get. Accepting a result does not mean being resigned to fate or giving up. Rather, it presents the opportunity to use that result to make a new decision that now has a chance to take our endeavor to the next level. This process is a progressive and constant cycle.

Humility allows us to drive, accept, and build. Channel your fear into driving toward your goal with all your energy, passion, and conviction. Expect to win and be successful. However, if you fail, give up the shame that accompanies it. Recognize and accept the outcome or results quickly. Realize that you now have new choices. Build on these new circumstances by assessing the new risks, and drive toward your next goal. This cycle will assist you in gaining confidence and will provide the best opportunity for the successful outcome you seek.

Robert Rubin, former U.S. Secretary of the Treasury, told graduates in the 2001 Harvard Commencement Address:

> Any individual decisions can be badly thought through, and yet be successful, or [decisions can be] exceedingly well thought through, but be unsuccessful, because the recognized possibility of failure in fact occurs. But over time, more thoughtful decision-making will lead to better overall results, and more thoughtful decision-making can be encouraged by evaluating decisions on how well they were made rather than on outcome.[2]

Unfortunately, in business we are obsessively focused on the outcome and the search for the cause related to that outcome, but, as William James said, "The word *cause* is an altar to an unknown god."[3] In other words, the *real* cause is almost impossible to find. Regardless, the bottom line has become more important than the process of getting there. This is because the results seem objective and relatively easy to assess and measure. But it is a mistake to think that all good outcomes are the result of good process.

One reason this can't be true is that luck and timing play such an important role. John Mayer, an award-winning American rock singer, put it this way: "Don't let my success validate the stupid decisions I have made in my life."[4] Luca Rigotti from Duke University's Fuqua School of Business agrees that "You can find correlations between the most improbable things . . . you'll just end up doing silly stuff."[5] Beth Kinney, who was tragically burned over a large percentage of her body when her stove exploded in her Newport Beach home in 2006, reminds us that, "This didn't have to happen for me to learn to change my life. But out of what happened, this is what I learned."[6]

By contrast, the best long-term performers in any probabilistic field—such as investing, sports team management, and pari-mutuel betting—all emphasize that good process will eventually lead to a good outcome.[7]

Edward Russo and Paul Schoemaker illustrate the process-versus-outcome paradigm by stating that as a result of probability, good decisions can lead to bad outcomes and bad decisions can lead to good outcomes (see Figure 10.1).[8] However, over the long run, the process of good decisions prevails over outcome.

Robert Rubin provides excellent principles for decision making based on process, not outcome.[9]

- "The only certainty is that there is no certainty." Research shows that people take too many risks and that they are over-confident in their prediction of the outcome. I can't repeat this too many times. Many businesspeople, especially entrepreneurs, risk far too much for the potential financial reward. They are blinded by passion, bravado, and ego, and driven by the archetypal myths discussed earlier in this book. Every businessperson needs to respect Lady Luck and the Three Sisters of Fate.

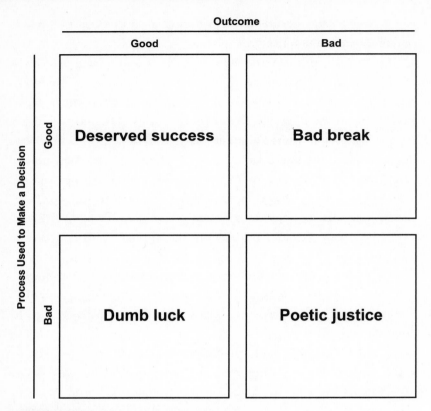

FIGURE 10.1 Process versus Outcome

■ "Despite uncertainty, we must act." Most decisions are based
on incomplete information. This is just the nature of business. We must make decisions on what to do next based on
the information we have and the information we do not
have. If we wait for all the information we need (or want) to
make a particular decision, we will be waiting a very long
time. Inaction will sink our boat. Besides, there is evidence
that even though we often believe that more information
provides a clearer picture of the future and improves our
decision making, in reality, additional information often only
confuses the decision-making process.

Researchers illustrated this point with a study of horse-race handicappers. They first asked the handicappers to make race predictions with five pieces of information. The researchers then asked the handicappers to make the same predictions with 10, 20, and 40 pieces of information for each horse in the race. Even though the handicappers gained little accuracy by using the additional information, their confidence in their predictive ability rose with the supplementary data.

■ "Judge decisions not only on results, but how they are made." Rubin believes that results are important, but he states that if we judge ourselves based only on the results, it will be a serious deterrent to taking the risks that may lead to the right decisions. We have seen this happen in different cultures that have a lower tolerance for failure. This is why it is so important to stay away from such finite and destructive language as the word *failure*. The failure label makes us feel horrible and shameful. It makes us more risk-averse and makes us want stop trying. It gives us heavy baggage that may prevent us from moving forward and accomplishing all that we are capable of accomplishing.

Valuing process over outcome is the seventh building band for gaining true business confidence.

Too often, we are entirely focused on the result. We often ask, "What did you get?" or "How did it end?" As businesspeople we are busy racing to the conclusion: Did we succeed or fail? But think about the best book that you have ever read. Was it the best book because of the ending? Or was it the best book because of the story that moved you along from one page to the next?

If we want to gain true business confidence and resiliency, what matters is not so much what happens at the end but the process that we go through. Examining and improving process and not just counting on outcome will lead to more business confidence. We will have confidence in the way we approach a business problem and then accept whatever outcome emerges.

When failure occurs, we must learn to view it as a new decision point and make the best decision we can from where we are. It does not matter that we fail or the number of times we fail, because if we continue with this cycle and use good process we will eventually reach the outcome we seek. As with the method employed by the *Gossamer Albatross,* iteration matters. It leads to much better decision making as a result of your experienced outcomes. From that process and outcome comes a new process and outcome. *Effort and effective process will eventually yield some brand of success.* Good process leads to good decision making, which will lead to more satisfaction.

Earning Your License to Fail

The value of your business experience may not be evident every day or every fiscal quarter. This is the struggle we face as businesspeople. We must set a series of small and longer-term goals that change based on the success and failure we achieve at each outcome point. Businesses change gradually overtime.

Sometimes it seems like we are standing still and other times the world shifts overnight. It is like the process that we all go through to catch a plane these days. Rush forward—no, wait; stop, go back, and then rush forward again. How do we cope with this lack of rhythm or predictable path?

We need to view piloting a business like navigating a sailboat across a windy lake (or a bouncing rubber band ball). Sailors cross lakes not by going straight to their destination point. The sails are set relative to the wind and to the direction you want to travel. Wind blowing directly from our destination makes the direct approach impossible. Instead, sailors use a method call *tacking*: They position the boat relative to the trim of the sails to allow them to sail to a closer point that gets them gradually nearer their goal. They sail in this zigzag manner, as close as possible on one side of the wind, then the other.[10] (See Figure 10.2.)

Making progress in business is very much like tacking in sailing. To cross the lake (or ocean, depending on what journey you are on), you need to follow the wind closely to the point where you can make progress. In business, this requires you to make a decision based on current facts (the direction of the wind) as you see and feel them. When you get the result (one tack point of progress), you make another set of decisions based on current facts (reading the wind again). A good definition of tacking is a course of action meant to minimize opposition

FIGURE 10.2   Lake Confidence: Tacking across the Lake

to the attainment of a goal. Similarly, in a ping-pong or tennis game, we can hit the bouncing ball where we think our opponent will not be, but we must return it from the place to which they hit it back.

Although perhaps not the straightest or quickest way to the goal, testing each outcome point in this way will be the best way to make progress toward a successful outcome.

This is similar to the path that Rex Grossman, quarterback of the Chicago Bears football team, traveled to take his team to the championship Super Bowl in 2007. During the season, Grossman's passer rating fluctuated from 0.0 to 137. He would have a great game followed by a terrible game, or a few bad or good games in a row. Nonetheless, this zigzag path took him to the championship game.

Steven Baird, CEO of Baird and Warner, the oldest real estate brokerage in the United States, says we need to learn that there is never a bad decision. His motto is that it was "a good point at a good time."

This is similar to the approach taken by Lisa Benham, a volunteer at Burners without Borders, an organization that helps where traditional social structures are failing. She states that "You just have to lean down and pick up one brick at a time. That's how anything ever [gets] done."[11]

I always loved what famous Yankee baseball manager Yogi Berra said: "When you come to a fork in the road, take it." Some may think this is ridiculous, but Berra was being profound. When you come to a decision point, take one route; just don't stay where you are.

Marsha McVickers, CEO of Errand Solutions in Chicago, sees herself as a gymnast when she fails.

> What happens to me is that if I fall down, my environment is still pretty much the same, but if I do a few somersaults to the other side of the room, my perspective has changed, and by changing that I can work through the challenges that came up during the failing process. I meet

with my advisers, and if I'm not able to somersault my way out of a certain situation, then they're able to tell me how to tuck and roll. It's a tremendous support system. If you're passionate and you're persistent and you surround yourself with a support system, friends and family, you can change any perspective from a failing one into one that will help grow and enhance your business.

CHAPTER 11

Goal Setting: Establishing Your Own Scorecard

By nature, most businesspeople seem to be driven to overcome obstacles. Many high achievers *enjoy* encountering barriers, perhaps even to the point of seeking out obstacles to scale and overcome. We especially love to knock over walls, ford rivers, and achieve the seemingly unachievable. "We have never found a mountain we did not want to climb" seems almost to be part of our national psyche. The conviction that we *must* conquer that mountain can just end up driving us crazy.

In 1962, when President John Kennedy committed America to go to the moon, he proclaimed, "But why, some say, the moon? Why choose this as our goal? And they may well ask why climb the highest mountain? Why, 35 years ago, fly the Atlantic? Why does Rice play Texas? We choose to go to the moon. We choose to go to the moon in this decade and do the other things, not because they are easy, but because they are hard."[1]

Kennedy Speech September 12, 1962

Sometimes, when we strive for lofty goals, we fail. What happens when, as Rabbi Harold Kushner wrote in his 2006 book, *Overcoming*

Life's Disappointments (Knopf, 2006), our dreams collide with reality to produce profound failure? What happens when life doesn't turn out the way we thought it would? Kushner suggests that we need to free ourselves from the "tyranny of the dream" because how we deal with the smashup of dreams and reality will determine our happiness.

One facet of this tyranny is the expectations that others have for us—our family, our bosses and employees, our investors, and especially our customers. There is nothing inherently wrong with having high hopes and large expectations, but what happens when life does not turn out the way you planned? We need to free ourselves from these expectations. We need to question, whose dream is it anyway?

Despite the tumultuous economic realities of today, most teens surveyed in 2006 through the Schwab Foundation believe they will be much more successful than their parents.[2] The promise of the next generation doing better in every way is seductive. I do this with my own children—I want them to be successful where I was not. While I wasn't good at sports growing up, my youngest son has a passion for it. I support his passion as a way to somehow to make up for my youthful failings. My wife was not good at math. She feels so proud when my oldest son gets 100 percent on his math test. It is natural for us to want better for those we love. Maybe so—but again, whose dream is it anyway, and what foundation are we really laying for the way our children look at themselves now and in the future?

Sometimes we can't choose our dream. However, even when our dream is thrust upon us, we can choose how to respond to it. We can also choose to find a new dream. David Myers, a professor of psychology at Hope College, suggests that "Happiness seems less a matter of getting what we want than wanting what we have."[3]

We need to stop replaying the Bill Gates and Michael Dell stories and the other success archetypes discussed earlier in this book. We are setting ourselves up by seeking other people's dreams. Now this is the wrong kind of crazy!

We are so afraid of failure and of truly testing ourselves that we conveniently (or maybe lazily) adapt to someone else's dream. But there is no shame in surrendering dreams that were thrust upon us when we were young. We need to develop our own dreams, based on who we are and what we want to achieve. Still, quitting can be a lot harder sometimes than keeping on. For better or worse, many of us were taught not to be quitters—taught that quitters are losers and that winners don't give up.

Make Progress via Intermediate Goals

If we build a dream filled with intermediate milestones, we can have intermediate successes. Remember, just as it is impossible to always succeed, it is also impossible always to fail, as long as we establish goals and define failure in the right way.

Intermediate goals also give us a way to tack to the next decision point—without having to set one of those impossible to predict (and usually to achieve) hockey stick–like trajectories to success. As I was completing this book, one of my favorite features in the Microsoft Word software became "Word Count," which I used to tell me how long the manuscript was and how much progress I was making toward my word goal each day. It is fine, great, even necessary to keep score. But how about playing a series of short games instead of one long game of life? Instead of trying to climb to the second floor by making a 20-foot leap from the lobby, how about climbing each step in the staircase? Of course, we have to remember that the business staircase probably doesn't just go up, but down and to the side as well, as depicted in Figure 11.1.

Linda Regulbutto uses dancing analogies to explain her nonlinear advancement. "Sometimes you go side to side for a while. There are a lot of good dance steps that happen side to side—the jitterbug and the marengo. Going side to side isn't too bad. It's okay to be still and let

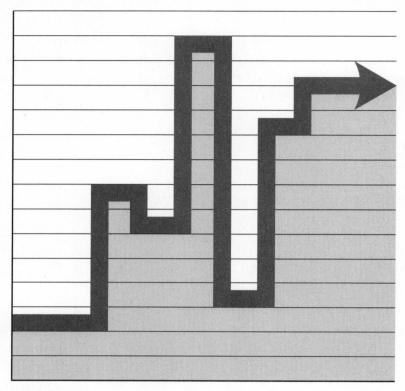

FIGURE 11.1   Stairway to Business Success

life happen, but don't stay there too long. Otherwise you'll be too
comfortable being uncomfortable."

Define the Goal before You Start: Striving for Minimal Achievement

Before setting out on a new outcome or path, define what success
and failure will be at this particular time. To do this requires the true
confidence to give up the archetype models of success and create
new models of our own. We must ask the same question I always ask

a new consulting client: "As we talk today, what will success look like when we get there?"

This allows two things. First, by defining success before we start, we can celebrate it when it occurs. Second, we will remember what success was supposed to mean. Too many times, when success becomes seemingly easy or quick, we grow greedy and want to push a particular process well past its intended outcome. As the old adage says, pigs have a tendency to get fat; hogs get slaughtered.

If we define success ahead of time, then it does not become a moving target, and we need not postpone feeling good about the success we have achieved. During the Internet bubble, I set certain target prices at which I would sell certain stocks. My gain would have been excellent. Then, as prices continued to climb, I kept raising my sell price, unwilling to miss out on any future gains. Many times I got greedy; most of the time, I got slaughtered.

We need to strive for minimal achievement in setting our immediate goals. I found this very useful later in my career while taking meditation. When I was learning from my Zen master, I asked simply, "How much I should meditate?" He told me that I should try meditating for a few minutes each week. After a few weeks of doing this, I came back to him and asked, "Now how much should I meditate, now that I have completed that task?" He told me I should try meditating a few minutes twice a week. If I was successful at that, I should add a third time. In this way, he told me, I could focus on not accomplishing too much when I started out, but in the long run I would be able to establish a routine that can achieve a meaningful goal of integrating meditation into my life.

The most popular time to join an exercise club in the United States is after January 1 of any new year. But most people who start a new exercise regimen burn out in just a few weeks because they try to do too much too fast.

The Go-Active chain says that of new gym members who have not previously belonged to a gym, 70 percent of those who start varying

from their established routine within the first six weeks will drop
out.[4] According to a 2003 study published in the *European Journal of
Sports Science,* up to 65 percent of new gym members drop their mem-
berships within the first six months.[5] This is why, in their economic
model, many gym clubs charge a high initiation fee, so that they can
make money even if you do not come back.

Jeff King, CEO of PSD Solutions in Chicago, says that he looks
at the small things on a daily basis. "You get a new account or positive feedback from a client. Those things help me build confidence."
Perhaps checking the accounts receivable report or e-mailing a client
to ask if they are satisfied with your service will be that small goal that
gives you confidence. For me, I might practice one part of my speech
to see how effectively I am delivering just that section, instead of
devoting the whole morning to practicing the entire speech.

Small successes come from getting feedback on the previous decision or set of decisions, which then enables us to look at the process
and increase the odds of a later, more positive result. Bob Sheldon,
founder of an industrial design firm, Product Council, describes these
small successes as "getting your toe wet and the next thing you know
you're diving in."

Patient Dreams

Patience is one of the biggest skills people lack; in today's society,
everything is "Need It Now!"[6] In our electronic, instant-message
world, immediate gratification is the standard. For my teenage son,
e-mail is too slow. Only text or instant messaging will do.

My younger son always wants to know why he can't have whatever he wants right now. If you can download software from the
Internet or have access to games right now, why not an instant
book or toy? He has wondered more than once why there is not
a chute or something similar on his computer where new physical
products could come out once he has ordered them. (I tell him that

we would need increased Internet bandwidth for that, and that he would need two part-time jobs!)

Actually, he isn't completely off. A version of instant delivery was attempted during the Internet bubble of 2001. A company named Kozmo delivered a limited amount of merchandise, from DVDs to Starbucks coffee, within one hour of ordering, 24 hours a day in Chicago. As I was putting my older son to bed at 8:30 P.M. the night before his tenth birthday, he said he sure hoped that I had remembered that he wanted a skateboard for his birthday. I left his room in a panic. I had forgotten.

I immediately ordered the skateboard (naturally, at a premium price) from Kozmo. It arrived 90 minutes later. I wrapped it and placed it near my son's bed so it would be there when he awoke. Unfortunately, as chronicled in the documentary *e-Dreams,* Kozmo was set to go public a month before the market crashed in 2001. They were out of business about a year later. My son still has that skateboard.

There are often good reasons that we are impatient. For example, we want to get more things done. The only way we think we can be more productive is to hyper-multitask. I can't remember the last time I was doing only one thing—even when I'm practicing meditation. (Let's hope my Zen master isn't reading this book.)

We talk on our cell phones and drive.[7] Right now, I am writing this book, listening to music, answering e-mails, monitoring instant messages, and replying to questions from one or both of my sons. Worse yet, I admit that I also answer e-mail while I drive. Maybe this multitasking was once a virtue, but today it's turned into frenetic juggling—frying our brains and detracting from good decision making.

According to Dr. Bruce Wiemer, a neurologist in Glendale, California, "You pay attention to task number one for a minute, put it aside and pay attention to task number two . . . you rapidly sequence."[8] Our brains are not an Intel dual-core processor. We can only do one thing, maybe two things well at a time. Dr. David Myer, at the University of Michigan states that multitasking impacts the speed and accuracy of the work that we are doing. "It is a myth that having many tasks going at once gets things done faster."[9]

This constant interruption is the enemy of productivity and performing well on a given task. Performing tasks serially may take longer and require more patience, but studies indicate that serial flow and focus become driving factors in getting the best outcome.

Some would make the case that patience is boring. But as German philosopher Walter Benjamin said, "Boredom is the dream bird that hatches the eggs of experience."[10] I have had some of my best ideas daydreaming on a long transatlantic airplane ride.

Rewind to 1995 when I first started taking Zen meditation. After one class, I complained to my Zen Master that my legs were uncomfortable sitting in zazen position.[11] He told me to try practicing in this position for two more years and if I was still uncomfortable, I should talk to him again. My Zen master had just presented me with a definition of patience that I could understand.

Matt McCall, managing director at DFJ Venture Partners in Chicago, describes patience as a key component for success in the business world:

> Often, it seems like an eternity as you wait for customer behavior to come around or for a market to take off. You do everything you can to keep the company afloat so that you don't get taken out during the drought. At some point, you begin to get up every morning wondering why you are doing this . . . the low salary, the fire drills and stress, the long hours and the frustration. And then, just when you've had enough, the market begins to come around. One customer buys, then another and another. Eventually, you are scaling rapidly and your issues turn to operational issues and efficiency.[12]

A lack of patience and the need for immediate gratification leads us to rely on the archetypes of success. Many times, this puts the ego in the lead, forces humility to go underground, raises the fear of immediate failure, and makes us take unnecessary risks. We give up our bounce.

Raising That White Flag: No Shame in Surrender

If we define failure ahead of time, we know when to stop pursuing certain paths; we know when to get out, and why to leave. Again, too many times, we think if we stay a bit longer or work a bit harder, we can turn it around. But as Will Rogers said, "If you find yourself in a hole, the first thing to do is stop diggin."

It is almost always a lot harder to quit than to keep going. So many of us stay past the time when a business or personal relationship is profitable, productive, or healthy. Part of the reason we stay may be that, by not having defined failure, we create the latitude to keep telling ourselves that we haven't failed yet. This is why defining success and failure up front helps us develop the kind of crazy confidence we need to rebound. Unlike what many of us believe, having the courage to quit can sometimes actually build more confidence then staying the course.

Deborah House says that we can't let "other people decide whether you failed and not." It bears repeating: Each of us must define what will constitute failure of a project or activity, before we begin. Then, when we are unable to change the outcome or we are not able to responsibly take the financial or emotional risks that pursuing the current course of action demands, we will know to quit. There is no shame in surrender.

Vince Lombardi, the famous football coach, said that "quitters never win and winners never quit." This is partially true. While determination and perseverance are good attributes to have in order to survive when our dreams do not come true, in business we find that winners actually know when to quit. Time and time again in business, the people who truly succeed knew when to get out, either because they wanted to savor the success they had achieved or because it was time to cut their losses, declare that sunk was sunk, and lick their wounds to live to see another day. If you fear failure too much, you will never be able to quit at the appropriate time, and will thus set yourself up for more failure, by whatever definition you chose.

Remember, unless you are in the underwater recovery business, what's sunk stays sunk. Money spent is not coming back. This is part of what *not* making fatal mistakes is all about—having enough energy and financial resources left to restart and go at the goal (or a different goal) from a different angle. Once you are bankrupt or broke, in many societies, you simply do not get another chance.

The most difficult decision a businessperson makes is to know whether they should keep their business going or shut it down. Many businesses make just enough money to generate just enough cash flow *not* to make this conclusion obvious. This is the ultimate measure of true business confidence—the ability to declare that something we have been trying to do is a failure, before anyone else declares it for us. We need to take that responsibility without waiting for someone else (the bank, clients, partners, whoever) to make the decision that we are unable to make.

Another version of this consideration is the question, should I stay or leave my current job? There are just enough good days to relieve the pain, and looking for a new job is just difficult enough not to make the decision a clear one. We are all creatures of habit. It is much more difficult to stop what we are doing and try something new than to just keep doing what we are doing. Admit it: Most of us suffer from inertia. The barriers to change are very high.

Jonathan Black, in his book, *Yes You Can!* cites a study about what makes people change, from the Family Institute in Evanston, Illinois.[12] This study states unequivocally that pain is still the best motivator to change.

Deborah House agrees that the biggest mistake most businesspeople make is that they don't stop what they are doing, or they continue to do the same thing. "So I tell them to stop—doing it harder or faster is not going to make it work—and take a step back and do something different."

In the early 1990s, I was selling voice-activated computer systems (similar to IBM's Via Voice) for a company I started called CompuVox. I traveled around the country and demonstrated a computer you could talk to. It was to be used in quality control and inventory. When I demonstrated it, everyone loved it. Everyone wanted to invest in the company, but no one bought the product. How come?

Change is difficult. Change is risky. It was much safer for my potential clients to continue with bar code that had been around for decades (although it had shortcomings that my new product addressed) than to risk their careers or future on something new. When I was at IBM, we always repeated the mantra, "No one got fired for buying IBM products," and then we cashed our checks.

By objectively defining failure and success before we start, we set up the metrics and measuring stick that tell us when to stop before we cause a fatal mistake to us and our business.

Setting patient goals for what success and failure will look like is the eighth building band on your path to true business confidence.

Having Too Much Will Make You Stupid

Everyone (except maybe the Donald Trump archetypes, whom we have by now given up on anyway) must eventually deal with limited resources. Accept it—limited resources are a fact of life.

Sometimes, we get into the "If only I had . . ." game, where we decide that if we only had this resource—skills, training, the right people, new intellectual property, or (the big one) more money—then our success would be guaranteed. This is delusional.

There will always be something you lack in your business. Except perhaps for baseball's New York Yankees, the perfect team does not exist (and even the Yankees don't win all the time). Such is the nature of a business world that thrives on supply and demand. It exists on the scarcity of some resources and the abundance of others. As American comedian Steven Wright jokes, "If you had everything, where would you put it?"[14]

Again, remember King Midas and the lottery winners, whose "everything" brought larger problems than they had before. Making a go of it with whatever resources you have at a particular point in time is the requirement for business success. Scarcity can be a competitive advantage and a barrier to entry that makes you more successful if you learn to operate lean and mean.

Furthermore, having too much can actually make you stupid. With an abundance of resource, we have a tendency to be lazy and throw resources and money at a problem instead of using our creativity. A business called Despair.com has a great poster about achievement. It depicts the Egyptian pyramids and states, "You can do anything you set your mind to when you have vision, determination, and an endless supply of expendable labor."

The old saying that "Necessity is the mother of invention" applies to every aspect of business. Accept where you are and the resources you have to get to your goal. At the next outcome point, things will be different. Your resources will probably change, and you will be faced with a different decision.

CHAPTER 12

No Longer Black and White: Measure for Success in Technicolor

Caution: The World Keeps Score and Numbers Lie

In Darwin's theory of evolution, nature only keeps score based on which members of the species are able to survive. It's the ultimate professional wrestling cage match. It's the World Series, the Tour De France, and the World Cup all rolled into one. Not all that many generations ago, physical survival was the only measure of success. In war, the army that lives gets to write the battle history. In sports, the team with the highest score at the end of the game has boasting rights. In boxing, the boxer left standing gets hands held high in the center of the ring.

The business world has always used money to keep score. Whoever has the biggest financial returns is the most successful and is declared the winner. Whoever loses money is declared a failure. It is that simple most of the time. In America, we do this because with so many different cultures and values, money is the common denominator. More homogeneous cultures are able to add other things to the definition of success.

For example, while financial success is important to the Japanese culture, they also place significant value on integrity and honor. Since the days when Samurai warriors killed themselves to keep from falling into the hands of the enemy, in business and life if something goes terrible wrong, Japanese commit hara-kiri or seppuku, ritual suicide in order to protect one's honor. I'm glad I'm in a culture that doesn't practice seppuku, but I do think we benefit when we find other ways besides money to evaluate our progress and worth.

Bob Okabe, managing director at RPX Group and of Japanese descent, further notes that the way American and Japanese companies react to crisis is different. "In the United States, blame is often limited to a senior manager who had direct knowledge of the problem; anyone above that level is generally assumed to be blameless. In fact, companies often takes steps to exempt C level executives from responsibility. In Japan, it is routine for company leaders to accept responsibility and resign regardless of whether they had direct involvement or knowledge of the problem."

Let's look at two recent examples, one from California and one from Japan.

When Apple Computer was recently tagged in the options backdating mess, CEO Steve Jobs remained in his position even though he signed off on some of the grants. Here's how the San Francisco Chronicle described it in an October 2006 article:

> Apple Computer Inc. issued a report today on the company's backdating of options grants, concluding that CEO Steve Jobs knew about the practice but did not personally benefit and was not aware of the accounting implications. In releasing details of its internal investigation, the Cupertino technology company said that longtime Apple executive and former chief financial officer Fred Anderson has resigned from its board of directors.[1]

By contrast, a recent *New York Times* article reported that the president and the chairperson of a Japanese brokerage house were resigning over an accounting irregularity in which they had no active involvement.

> The Japanese brokerage firm, the Nikko Cordial Corporation, said Monday that its two most senior executives would resign because of accounting irregularities. The company said its president, Junichi Arimura, and its chairman, Masashi Kaneko, would leave on Tuesday, and that a director, Shoji Kuwashima, would become president. "We have no choice but to accept the view that we systematically reported fraudulent" figures, Mr. Arimura said. "I would like to offer my heartfelt apologies."[2] [The use of personal "heartfelt apologies" shows wounded integrity and honor in the Japanese culture.]

Paul Stiles, in his book, *Is the American Dream Killing Us?* states that we use money because it is the only "central organizing principle" we have. The market has its own hierarchy where the more money you have, the more elevated your position is.

> Success in America is neither moral or spiritual nor intellectual nor artistic these days, but financial. Unsure of what they stand for, people rely on money as the criterion for value . . . people deserve respect and admiration because they are rich. What used to be a medium of exchange has usurped the place of fundamental values . . . the cult of success has replaced a belief in principles."[3]

A Pew Research Center study shows that 80 percent of 19- to 25-year-olds see getting rich as a top life goal for their generation. Next in line were being famous (51 percent), helping the needy (30 percent), and being a leader (22 percent).[4]

It is far easier to keep track of how we are doing by a seemingly objective numeric score than to try to evaluate results based on qualitative measurements. This bias is becoming worse as computers give us an increasing ability to track and analyze just about everything. We are uncomfortable with any ambiguous method and try to reduce everything to a number because numbers are, after all, much easier to compare.

But numbers are far from infallible. Adam Galinsky, a professor at Northwestern University Kellogg School who specializes in management and organizations, states that not all numbers are even weighed equally in decisions. "People tend jump to conclusions based on the first numbers they hear and don't even allow later figures to change their minds."[5]

Numbers make us overconfident. In real business life, success and failure are not that black and white. The lines are much more blurry because something that seems like a failure when viewed through the prism of numbers now, may be very successful a year hence.

Alternately, it may look like our business is making a lot of money, but in the long run the company does not have financial staying power because our cost of sales is too high, or our competitor comes out with a new product that wallops us, our largest client moves off-shore— or our officers and accountants are cooking the books. Numbers can and do lie.

The Equation Starts with the Score

Don't get me wrong, I am all for keeping score. This is part of the fun in business and in sports. Did we win or lose? When my sons were introduced to baseball and soccer as small boys, the leagues were prohibited from keeping score in many games because they did not want the children to become too competitive. League leaders wanted to emphasize playing the game and having fun over winning or losing.

I think this is wrong. All the children on the team were keeping score anyway. They knew who was winning! More importantly, part of the game is learning how to win and how to lose. What does each feel like? In winning, we can celebrate with our team members that we did a great job. We are elated because we worked hard or just got lucky. In losing, we can console ourselves with our team members, learn what we can do better, shake it off, and vow to return the next day to try again. If we are going to build true business confidence, we have to know if we won or lost; we have to experience the feelings of both.

As in sports, those of us in business have to expect to have our winners and losers declared. It is important to celebrate our victories and lick our wounds after our defeats. Keeping score should be part of every equation measuring success. But the money score can't be the only term in the equation.

Can't Money Buy at Least a Little Happiness?

We also keep score with money because we think it buys happiness. David Myers retorts that the American dream has now become "life, liberty, and the purchase of happiness."[6] A Lexus ad promises that "Whoever said money can't buy happiness isn't spending it right"[7]

Barry Schwartz, in his book *The Paradox of Choice* (Ecco, 2004), describes how the accumulation of possessions is really detrimental to our wellness and produces stress and anxiety. "People can never relax and enjoy what they have already achieved. At times, they have to stay alert for the next big chance."[8] As Jonathan Black writes in *Yes You Can!* at one point in 2004, there were 24 television shows running about home improvement. "We call in the queer guys to help with our closets and wine cellars. We entrust our out-of-control children to an English nanny . . . nothing is impossible to fix. We could even swap our spouses! The ABC television show *Wife Swap* gets an average of 250 calls a week from people who'd like to switch homes."[9]

Paul Stiles cites two indicators that show that we spend all the money we make to "keep up with the Joneses." First, since the 1980s, American personal savings rates have been going down until it is only about 3 percent, a fraction of what other industrialized nations save.[10] In 1999, Stiles states, the lowest third of Americans had no savings and the middle third had less than $3,000. More importantly, during the bull market of the 1990s, when personal income was rising faster than in many other periods in history, credit card debt tripled.[11]

This has been great for market productivity because people believe that the harder they work, the more money they will make and the happier they will become. However, Stiles cites studies that show that money only buys happiness "up to a certain point, the point at which one has lifted oneself out of poverty. But once you have clothes on your back, a roof over your head, and food on your table, multiple sources suggest that all the money in the world is not going to make you one bit happier"[12]

Stiles points out that, ironically, beyond a certain point money actually buys unhappiness. "Once you have achieved a basic standard of material well being, happiness comes from family and friends, marriage, leisure activities, and the nature of your work. These things are all negatively impacted by the excessive pursuit of money which creates stress, steals family time, alters moods, and breeds friction . . ."[13]

Myers points out that "in countries where nearly everyone can afford life's necessities, increasing affluence matters surprisingly little."[14] In 1957, Americans' average income was $8,700. Today, it has more than doubled to $20,000.[15] Are we twice as happy? Myers cites statistics that say we are not. Divorce has also doubled, suicide tripled, violent crime quadrupled, and depression is an epidemic. "When it comes to psychological well being, it is not the economy, stupid."[16] Remember the research discussed earlier that lottery winners were not happier eight weeks after winning the lottery?

This overachievement culture is also having a profound effect on our children. Erika Schickel, in her September 2006 review of books that looked at problems regarding how parents push their children to succeed, wrote, "We have just succeeded in minting our first generation of superior beings and indeed, these young adults are driven, highly educated, and skilled in many arenas. Many of them have found professional and financial success. But they are also too exhausted, lonely, confused, drug addicted, and dispassionate to enjoy the rewards."[17]

Being higher up on Maslow's hierarchy of needs may be over-rated. There are many third world economic cultures that focus on basic everyday needs. Did we feed our family today? Were we able to get shelter from the elements? Did we sleep under a roof? Success in these environments is measured daily. These short-term goals and successes might provide a lot more satisfaction then some of the long-term, impossible, or unquantifiable goals that many of us seek.

If we focused on the basic necessities of food and shelter instead of always trying to figure out what each business decision and stage means, we might be able to enjoy more fulfilling if simpler lives. This would provide the short-term successes that we need on which to build true business confidence. It would also provide us an easy mechanism to let go of past failures, since the next day would bring the immediate challenges of getting food and shelter. We wouldn't have the luxury of wallowing in the previous day's failure. We would focus on food for tomorrow and shelter for tonight.

Almost none of us will agree that it would be a great idea to pack up our families tomorrow to move to a more basic economic culture. But the thought of it is a way of learning to focus on small, immediate goals and success and not get weighed down in pondering what it all means for my future and what impact it will have on my life every single day. It is a way to appreciate the success we had today, or a way to make us let go of the failure we had yesterday and try for a different or new outcome today. This is why various team-building activities have become popular, such as wilderness retreats for company managers or employees. They get to focus on attaining short-term goals together—like climbing a steep cliff.

International Goal Setting

Different cultures set different life goals. In New Zealand, it is not all about success and failure. It is about the lifestyle that the businessperson wants to create. New Zealand business owners have struck a work–life balance. This is particularly true of Rory and Sandra Burke, who own Burke Publishing. They operate their business from their sailboat, the *Pacific Voyager*.

> It's a fabulous lifestyle, but one that severely limits their company's growth potential. To really ramp up sales, Rory says, they'd need to dry-dock the boat, move to a land-based office, and start hiring employees. And to the Burkes, that sounds like a lousy tradeoff. "We're lifestyle entrepreneurs," Rory says. "We try to strike the balance between income, possessions, the time we work, and where we work." If that means Burke Publishing remains the same size, that's okay with them.[18]

When I presented in Palmerston North on the North Island of New Zealand in the summer of 2006, most business participants only had three goals in life: to have a boat, a BMW, and a summer house.

> Experts say that an annual income that is the equivalent of just $70,000 in the United States is considered the pinnacle of economic achievement in New Zealand. As a result, few businesses have American-style expansion plans. By one count, the entire country, with a population of four million, has just 240 businesses that employ more than 500 workers.[19]

Your Second Goal: Money Plus

We would be well served to blur the lines and not be focused only on money and financial results. Results need to be viewed in a continuum with many features and not just a single monolithic outcome; real results are Technicolor, not black and white.

Read and track the income statement and balance sheet of your business. But measure the results in additional ways that are not in the accounting system in your company's computer. Ask the following "*and*" questions, and then add your answers to your company's financial score to come up with a total index of your success.

Perspective

■ From today's perspective, did the business win or lose against your original definition of what success and failure look like?

■ *And* from tomorrow's, or next week's, or next month's perspective, did the business win or lose?

Other Outcomes

■ *And* are there any lower-priority successes that you actually achieved? Did you get any other return on your investment besides the monetary one? Did you learn something more about your competition? Did your people receive some on-the-job training that will benefit down the road? Did you find a new use for an old technology?

■ *And* can you use those results to pursue a course that will make success more likely next time? How—automatically, or will you have to invest a little more?

Personally Speaking

■ *And* can you learn anything from this latest result about yourself, your business, the industry, or your customers? This is in addition to the outcome. You may have received a poor outcome, but if you learned anything in these other categories, it will help your future decision-making process.

■ *And* this time did you separate your personal goals from those of your business? Did you let your ego get in the way? What are your personal goals that don't mimic anyone else's? Did you exercise your humility?

■ *And* how long did you wallow in your latest setback this time? Was it shorter than last time? *And* how long did it take you to realize that you have been in the trough of failure before and that this, too, will pass?

- *And* can you hold on to these uncomfortable pieces of failure, doubt, and shame to begin yet another path? *And* can you remember this setback and still move on to other opportunities?

- *And* did you show progress or are you just evaluating the results, looking at the process, and plotting the next immediate move?

- *And* were you able to keep your sense of humor regardless of what happened? If we don't laugh in life, we end up crying.

Outside of You

- *And* to whom did you reach out to get help and advice after this latest result to figure out where to go next? Can you use them again?

- *And* to whom do you give credit, besides yourself, for this latest success?

After you have asked these questions of yourself, ask your business the questions in the following subsections. Beyond the financial statements—which, as we all know, can for a time mask other truths—these questions will help provide additional ways to measure success and failure.

Turn Around and Face Your Team

Did you make progress leading your team to a different place than in the past? Do you have a better understanding of what you need to do next from this different vantage point?

You may not be on higher ground, but this new point of view has given you information so that you can take whatever the next step is and have more of a chance to succeed from that place. A team that has both succeeded and failed together will produce better results. What did you learn about your team? What did they learn about you? What changes do you need to make in your team? Should some people leave? Should some people be given more responsibility?

Do the Numbers Lie?

Have you been able to accurately measure and report your results financially on a monthly basis? I learned the importance of this when I failed to conduct due diligence on the buying company in the sale of my last one. It cost me dearly. Do you understand every number on the income statement, balance sheet, and cash flow statement? Do you understand their relationships? Never, never, *never* leave this up to your financial adviser or controller.

The income statement says you made money (assuming there is a positive number at the bottom). Is this on a cash or accrual basis? Remember that cash is king. (The transaction is not over until the check clears the bank.) Do you have cash on your balance sheet? Is your quick ratio (current assets to current liabilities) at least greater than one?

Do you send invoices on time? Are your receivables all current? Clients who don't pay on time are not good clients; they are collection problems. Find out if their lateness is because they are dissatisfied with your product or service, or if they are chronic deadbeats. People respect what you inspect, as the old business adage says.

Can and do you pay all your bills in a timely fashion? Have you saved cash for covered operating expenses if business slows down?

The answers to *all* these questions determine the financial success and failure of our business. Over the years, we have seen a lot of businesses make money on their income statements, only to be deemed insolvent because of the financial sleight of hand that they employed in manipulating their statements.

Have You Neglected the Intangibles?

Do you regularly measure employee morale, the effects your competitors have on your business or the market place, or changes in your clients' preferences?

Show Me the Customers

Besides hitting your revenue targets, have you created a sales culture where everyone sells? New businesses especially need to take every opportunity to sell to customers, because the competitors are. Are you focused on the clients' pain and the people who pay for that pain and can pay you to solve it?

Do your customers return, or do you lose customers as fast as you gain them? Business is about repeat customers who keep buying from you over the long term. If you don't have customers, you have inventory and debt. If you don't have customers, it's a hobby, not a business.

Track Me Down

Do you have some type of customer relationship management system? How well do you use it to track and market to your clients over a long period of time? This becomes critical because we can't sell just anything to anyone at any time; we need to be there when they are ready to buy—or we need to be at the top of their mind so that they call us.

Customer relationship management systems allow you to do just this. A sales funnel of suspects, prospects, and repeat clients will also help you match your prospecting and closing patterns to help you forecast that all-important cash flow.

Excellent Service

Do you consistently give excellent customer service as a rule? This will keep clients coming back, which is critical to the success of your business.

However, this is a difficult one. Excellent customer service is dead in much of the world. This is ironic because, for the most part, the best competitive advantage any of us has is our excellent customer service. I tell my clients over and over to give good customer service and no one will get hurt. In most businesses, there is a great barrier to exit once you have the customer. Give great service and your customers won't try to find a way out of it—even if someone comes along with a better price.

Big Margins

Do you know your gross margins by product or line?

When my younger son was eight years old, he decided to start his own business by putting a price tag on everything he had in his room (everything we had bought for him). When guests came to the house, he would invite them up to his room, which now looked like a retail store, and try to sell them his merchandise.

One Saturday, I purchased my son an action figure for $5.00 at one of the big-box stores. When we arrived home, he immediately ran upstairs to his room and placed a $3.00 price on it. Seeing this, I decided to give him a little lesson in how business is done. I told him that no businessperson willing sells inventory for less than cost—especially on the first day the item hits the shelves. That meant, I explained, that he could not sell the action toy at $3.00 since it had just cost me $5.00. My son looked up at me and said, "It wasn't my five dollars. This toy didn't cost me anything."

He didn't need me to explain to him the concept of cost of goods sold—he already understood it perfectly. Since his cost was zero, he could sell the toy at any price and still make a good margin!

Understanding your gross margin is vital. It is easier to make money when 80 percent gross margins are 80 percent than when they are 20 percent, but a well-managed business can make money on margins as low as 2 percent. Are you categorizing all of your variable costs so you truly understand what it costs to make or supply your product?

Sales can be high, but if gross margins aren't, it will take a lot longer to earn the profits you seek. We are all reminded of the joke about two guys who bought potatoes for $1.00 and then sold them for $1.00. When one asked why they didn't make any money, the other replied that they needed a bigger truck!

Lower Fixed Costs

Are you cheap? Spend no dollar before its time. This does not mean that we should not invest in our business, but low monthly fixed costs keep businesses flexible during the tough times that will eventually come. Big rents, large staffs, and huge equipment lease payments limit flexibility.

Ask the Hard Question

And finally, don't be afraid to ask *the_*question. According to Fred Reichheld, who wrote the book *The Ultimate Question* (Harvard Business School Press, 2006), the only question you ever need to ask is, "Would you recommend us to a friend or colleague?"

With this, he created a Net Promoter Score (NPS), which takes the percentage of customers who are promoters (those who are highly likely to recommend your company) and subtracts the percentage who are detractors (those who are less likely to recommend your company). Therefore, the company's NPS is calculated as follows:

$$\% \text{ of Promoters} - \% \text{ of Detractors} = \text{Net Promoter Score}$$

In the long run, a high NPS will guarantee financial success. Customers will come back to you, and they will refer other people. Referrals are the best and least expensive business development tool you have.

Money and Fun

Mark Jepsen, an owner at Machete, a commercial editing company, believes that all work is a combination of making money and having fun. He looks at his work from four different angles, as displayed in Figure 12.1, and recommends that we identify which combination a particular piece of business is.

The ideal place for most of us to be is the upper right corner, "Make money, have fun." This is what we all want—to make money and really enjoy doing it. The worst place to be is where you are having "No fun, no money," but there it is also easy to walk away. Alternately, many people have a place for pro bono work in their life

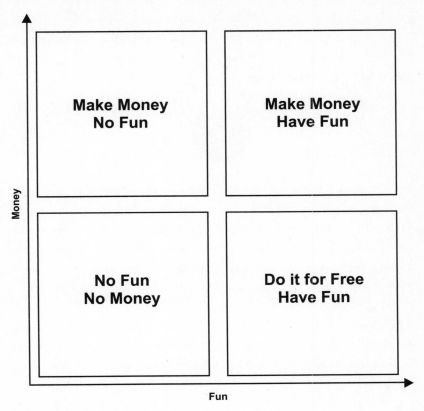

FIGURE 12.1 Money and Fun

where they are doing it for free, but it really is fun so they continue to participate.

The most difficult place to walk away from is the upper left quadrant, where you are making money but having no fun. I once had a difficult client for two years from whom I was unable to walk away because they paid *too* well. Every week, this one day of misery supported what I wanted to do the other four days, which in 2002 was writing my first book. But once I finished my book, I quit the client and walked away. I have met many people who are miserable in their jobs but stay because they think they make too much money to leave. That's why employers pay people a lot of money for really bad jobs.

Passing Your Own Test

By all means, keep score and make money. But setting up your own measures of success and failure and what they mean to you frees you from benchmarking against ambiguous or misleading indications from society or other people. The only test you need to pass is your own. Measure only what success means to you. *Creating your own measurement systems for success* that measure more than money is the ninth building band toward true business confidence.

My local dry cleaner is run by Mrs. Park, who came here from Korea. When I visit with my two sons, she always tells me, "Mr. Moltz, you are a very rich man," and I know she isn't talking about the labels in my shirts.

Many of us feel the same way that Kevin Turner at Modelmetrics does. He measures success through "self-actualization; realizing what I wanted to accomplish and achieving it; feeling good about my work and what is it that I do; having a positive impact on people that I work with and work for, as far as clients and businesses that hire us to do work for them; and then of course there's money."

One of the promotional quotes from the 2006 Chinese movie *Fearless* is from Lao Tzu: "Mastering others is a strength. Mastering yourself makes you fearless." For me, this means that the only test we need to pass is our own.

In business, beating others may show financial strength, but if we can understand ourselves, this can make us even stronger for times that we financially lose. We won't be affected as much by what others think and do. Rather than merely reacting to the environment, we will look within ourselves for understanding and direction.

Satisfaction as Success

Recent studies have shown that the most satisfying life experiences stem from the fulfillment of the top four human psychological needs: autonomy, competence, relatedness, and self-esteem. In virtually all cases, those whose experiences meet these top four needs are happier than those whose experiences do not. Other needs, including physical thriving, security, meaning, and pleasure, rank lower in importance but are still necessary for fulfillment. Ranking at the bottom of the scale? Money and luxury.[20]

How else can we ultimately define our own success if we don't want money to be the only metric? Each of us must answer this for ourselves; here's a way to start to get at it.

If you never get to that pot of gold at the rainbow, will the trip have been worthless? If so, what would make the trip worthwhile? What would you have wanted to achieve? Keep at it, and you will find something that really resonates for you. Looking at your passion is a place to start. How much fuel and satisfaction does that provide to you?

There's only one rule to this exercise: Even though the rest of the world has told you that it intends to measure you by how much money you make, and as a businessperson you accept the necessity of making money, in your quest for bounce you have to stop using money as a metric. It's a given. After all, we are talking about capitalism, not an artistic or charitable venture.

Now what else is a bona fide measure for you? Hopefully there is room for those things in your life as well. But in business, it should be money (profits and returns to investors) plus at least one other thing. This will give you balance and bounce as you progress toward your goals. It might be saving lives by developing a breakthrough drug;

saving the environment by finding innovative sources of fuel; creating new jobs in your region; or building something from nothing—this list could go on for pages.

Marsha McVicker, who runs Errand Solutions, depicts her company as helping both clients and employees at the same time: "The fact that I'm making 60 employees happy—quite honestly, they're making themselves happy; this is an organization where you make of it what you will—the fact they're finding this work rewarding gives me the courage to continue. My clients are amazing . . . when you give people back all this time [by doing their errands], you're impacting their lives at such a positive level, it's tremendously rewarding."

There will be successes and failures between this company and its clients, but each gets a reward and both sides can make continued progress toward satisfying their own goals. The employees will continue to be able to support their families by doing something they enjoy. The clients will continue to receive a service (getting errands done for them) that will enable them to add to the quality of their lives.

What keeps Tracy Thirion going is her belief in bigger ideas that can change the way things are done. She wants to "help people on our own terms, with more humanity, with hard work being rewarded in a lot of different ways." Anna Belyaev believes that we all need to create a living by "doing honest work. I lived in Russia for a while when the economy was falling apart and nobody had jobs. If paying work isn't there, things get really bad/crazy. Knowing that somebody has to take responsibility for that—the quality of life we want won't happen—makes me want to help."

Small Is the New Big Success Story

Success to Jay Goltz was to let go of building a $100 million business. His goal was to "get small."[21]

I met Jay in the late 1990s when I joined his group of entrepreneurs who met monthly to share ideas. Jay had been successfully growing his main businesses, Chicago Art Source and Artists' Frame Service, for almost 30 years, but he never saw himself as successful because he was always striving to make his business bigger.

He did not realize that business does not always have to entail fast-paced growth; that calm, controlled growth is good—better, even, because forcing the fast-paced growth could be reckless. He thought that, in order to be happy, he had to have "phenomenal growth" and to make his business into a huge company.

Now he realizes that he was wrong, and he has become much more involved in the management of his company. Now he not only loves going to work for the "exciting, fast-paced, creative energy part of it," but also for the "greater community sense that we're all on the same mission together. . . . For me, happiness is not about building a $100 million company."[22]

Will Harris runs his family farm, White Oak Pastures. His family has raised cattle on the same Early County, Georgia, farm for five generations. He never saw it as a big business, but he has made his contribution. "I think there's a lot wrong with the adult factory food system, there are a lot of excesses, and I really feel like I'm part of a bit of a movement that will be a benefit to consumers, to the land, to the cattle, and help rebuild the American factory farm systems. I'm not trying to sound like a crusader—I'm just a little foot soldier, but I'm happy to be part of that movement."

Finally, in one of my favorite movies of all time, *Jerry Maguire*, Tom Cruise's character listens to his mentor, Dickie Fox, who tells him, "Hey . . . I don't have all the answers. In life, to be honest, I have failed as much as I have succeeded. But I love my wife. I love my life. And I wish you my kind of success."

CHAPTER 13

Read This Book—Then Throw It Away

In the southwestern part of the United States there is a wonderful expression: "Big hat, no cattle." This means that some people can dress up and look the part of rancher, but that it's all an act.

In the Midwest, we say that some people are "all talk, no action." I am a Monday morning quarterback. I love to talk about the Sunday football games and what *I* would have done to win a particular contest, but you won't find me playing even a game of touch. As businesspeople, we love telling people what we would have done if only we were in their position—the accuracy of hindsight is always 20/20.

At one point in my life, I was a motivational book addict. I would read the books, listen to the tapes, and travel to every seminar that I could find and afford (and even some I couldn't). I never met a motivational quote I didn't like. I posted these positive aphorisms all around my apartment and office because I thought it gave me the confidence to be positive and motivated. But I was also pretending to live a happy business life since I was planning to do something great.

Planning to do things is the easy part. By only planning, I never had to be tested against true market conditions. Planning never gave me true business confidence. I never had to see if my product really worked. I never had to risk rejection from a prospect who did not want to buy my product or did not like it when they purchased it. I never had the pressure of paying vendors or meeting payroll. I never had to bounce.

Unfortunately, planning ultimately is not very profitable since you can't spend the money you plan to make (although some of us do go into debt spending money we do not have). In the Foreword to *The Complete Idiot's Guide to Business Plans,* I wrote that "business plans are meaningless."[1] By that I mean that the actual planning document that a businessperson ends up with really means very little. However, the process one goes through to formulate the business plan and then go out and get real customers is very worthwhile. Again, the *process* is where the learning is, not in some document that's going to be out-of-date in 90 days anyway.

Out of fear, we wait many times for the perfect moment when things are just right to launch a business or make a major decision. We wait for the planets to align, for the day we will have enough capital, the right team, the right market conditions, reliable customers, or downtrodden competitors.

Many would-be entrepreneurs I have met are waiting like this. Some of them will never be ready to take the leap. They are actually in a different kind of business. They are in the business of *planning to start a business.* They have the financial resources to sustain this since there never is any expense from the business if they never start it. It is much more comfortable to pretend to start a business then to get it all messed up or delayed by talking to customers to see if anyone will actual buy our product or service. By planning a business instead of actually starting one, we can avoid having to deal with rejection and other sticky issues.

This situation is similar to being a perpetual student and never going out and getting a job. Perpetual students are always in a training process, never quite believing they have enough education to get that perfect job that they want. Intrinsically, there is nothing wrong with either of these situations if planning or going to school is our ultimate goal in life. However, assuming our goal is something else, perpetual planning or endless training won't get us there.

Perfection Happens Only in Hollywood

The perfect moment in real business doesn't exist. I started my second business right after I got married: bad idea. I started my third business two weeks after my first son was born: worse idea. We don't get to choose the right time to make our next decision based on the process and outcome. If we did, we might be waiting forever and never move from where we currently are.

Waiting passively is a waste of time. We need to choose to do something, or even *choose* to do nothing, by making our decisions proactively. This is not the same as just waiting. After reviewing the process, we may proactively decide to wait. We might still do nothing, but our doing nothing is deliberate. Our basis needs to be some form of proactive decision instead of just reading books, going to seminars, or listening to educational audios. In reality, we are choosing all the time, even by not choosing. As Jean Paul Sartre said, "What is not possible is not to choose."[2]

Books can give you ideas, and motivational seminars do have their place—my boys do want to go college, after all. Writers and speakers collect and pass along information that generates new ideas and perspectives. Seminars and events can temporarily lift our audiences and readers up when they are down, but nothing replaces real-world experience where business people can exercise decision-making ability and business judgments by examining process and outcome.

While books, seminars, and other methods of learning can be valuable, be sure not to use them to feed fear or as an excuse to avoid taking appropriate risks. I hear all the time from businesspeople that they don't want to make decisions too early, before they have enough knowledge and experience to do it effectively. Surprise! None of us do. Most all of us only guess what is right based on the facts as we know them and on our past experience. Don't think of the decision as right or wrong. Think of it as simply the next_decision to make, based on where and how matters are now.

It's not the data or the training to make decisions that we need in order to be effective businesspeople, no matter what we've been told before. It's the process underneath that allows us to iterate through decisions and choices to make our way toward our goals with bounce.

We don't develop the true confidence to make creative decisions by staying safely in the foxhole, warming the bench, or choosing a seat in the back of the class. Philip Humbert, an author and motivational speaker, states in his newsletter, that "to succeed, you have to get in the game. You have to be willing to be a beginner, a novice, an amateur, even a fool. You have to start, and in the beginning, others with more experience, greater resources or talent may 'beat' you. You may 'lose.'" Humbert proclaims that by being in the game, you learn by getting results. Results typically gives you experience, wisdom, and sometimes even insight.

Fear is closely tied to courage. Helen Keller, the famous American blind and deaf educator said it well: "Life is either a daring adventure or nothing. Security does not exist in nature, nor do the children of men as a whole experience it. Avoiding danger is no safer in the long run than exposure."[3]

Preparation is important. Sometimes I wish we were able to accomplish our goals simply by thinking of them, but then I remember the satisfying rush of being in the middle of the fight. I remember what it is like to build a business out of nothing. I remember a great sales call or standing up in front of 2,000 people and experiencing their laughter and applause. I especially remember what it feels like to do all of these things after failing at them multiple times. By doing, we can gain the courage that comes from experiencing the business cycles of succeeding and failing. Eventually, this cycle will sustain us through failure and success.

Find the Key, Pick Up the Water, and What Is the Rod For?

As a teenager in 1977, the first video games I ever played were called Adventure, Star Trek, and Wompus. In those early video game days, they were more like interactive text games than today's video games; there were no graphics, just a dark screen and a cursor to enter commands.[4]

In Adventure[5] each command told the computer where you wanted to go. Players stumbled around in a cave and over an object, and then you had to intuit that you should pick the object up and do something with it. After playing the game for a while, we started to learn what the maze of the cave was all about. We knew what to pick up and what to leave on the ground. Most first-time players knew to pick up a key, but many did not know to pick up water until they had played the game for a while. (Remember, the screen was dark, and the only thing a player could see was very short text responses—almost like being in black screen mode today.) We learned where the entrance of the cave was and how not to get killed by the dwarf. We learned how to catch the plover (and what it was—a bird), to get past the snake, and what to do with the rod.

This is what building resiliency and understanding the foundations of true confidence is all about: knowing what to take, what to avoid, what to examine and leave where it is, or what to never pick up or even touch because it will prove to be a fatal business failure. We learn this through following our own unique paths (sometimes, like Adventure, in the dark) and by developing the skills along the way.

After reading this book, pick up each building band, recognize what it is, and use for your own rubber band ball, or discard it.

You will develop an intuition for recognizing these bands, which will be a more powerful learning tool than any "ten steps to success" you can struggle to apply to your particular journey.

Whatever our goals are, making better decisions leads to more success. The tenth and final building band is to *value action*—almost any action. Active decisions will lead to a bounce and a natural flow of your business life. Anything that gets in the way of a person making better decisions should be tossed overboard.

The ten foundations in business confidence lead to better decisions. Knowing to pick up the water, the plover, *and* the key leads to better decisions and a happier business life. Improve the way you make decisions, and you'll bounce. That's how to live life the way life was intended, and to achieve success in business or whatever your life work is.

Afterword

Lifelong Practice: Hitting for the Cycle

One of the most difficult achievements in baseball is to *hit for the cycle*. This means a player gets a single, a double, a triple, and a home run, all in one game, which demonstrates that the player in this game had consistent success each time at bat. This is analogous to the serial entrepreneur who is not satisfied with selling one company, but continues to start, succeed, fail, and sell many companies in succession.

Business is a lifelong practice. This is a difficult concept for many of us to grasp.

In my Seido Karate practice, we have one *kata,* a prearranged series of moves, called Geksai Dai. It is part of the *Makuso* or meditation katas. *Geksai Dai,* translated from the Japanese, literally means "breaking down the large fortress."

I wondered many times why my peaceful style of karate would have a kata with such a combative name. I came to understand that what we focus on while doing these series of moves is actually how long it takes to correctly and confidently perform all of them—similar to just how long it might take to actually break down a large fortress. Each time one of my karate teachers instructs us in the next thing to do, we say as acknowledgement, "Osu," an abbreviation of the Japanese word *oshinobu,* which means to strive with patience.

As I have discussed previously, patience is a lost art. We are in too much of a rush to get to the end and define our achievement. We are too concerned with our own personal velocity. We want to hit the home run our very first time at bat. We are just not satisfied with getting one base but want that home run.

We are convinced that at the end of the rainbow there is a pot of gold just waiting if we only can get there today. I have climbed to the top of the Sydney Harbor Bay Bridge and seen all 270 degrees of a rainbow. After a driving rain, it does look beautiful when you get there. But I did not see any pot of gold, at least not one with *Barry Moltz* written on it.

We are in a rush to accumulate as much gold as possible so we can show it off to others. Even though it may not buy happiness, we use our gold's shine to feel good about ourselves. We want to be our own version of King Midas. We frantically seek the reward that society has told us is waiting if only we are smart enough or work hard enough. Unfortunately, the gold will not replace the confidence that we desperately need to feel inside to ensure we achieve our level of success.

Although it is critical to have that grand, passionate vision to keep us moving on cold and stark days, the actual reward in business will be found simply in realizing a value in each outcome that visits us, whether favorable or not. This is the reward of approaching each day with true business confidence.

If you, like me, are part of the American business culture, recognize that this cultural environment does not really support failure, so we have to develop that support within ourselves.

Examining our decision process and facing outcomes with humility and candor will give us the bounce to go at it again. It will give us the kind of true business confidence we need in order to face whatever comes next. It will allow us to get our fear flying in formation.

We will appreciate our small successes and let go of those shameful failures. We will begin to understand that regardless of the outcome, we do have a choice. We will become better risk takers. This will eventually, over our business lifetimes, lead to the type of success we seek: money as well as the other, equally important parts of success.

Summary: The Ten Building Bands for True Business Confidence

1. *Environment.* Just like your parents said, it matters where we come from. Culture shapes our individual tolerance for success and failure. Each culture's archetypes of success teach how others define it and the pressure that comes with that definition. Archetypes drive us the bad kind of crazy and hold us back.

2. *Humility.* Forget the fairy tales. Our business careers are not linear. Life changes very quickly and bad times will happen. We all screw up sometimes. Randomness and luck play a large role in financial success. Use humility to right-size your ego.

3. *Face the Fear of Failure.* Failure is an option, a good one in fact. It is okay to be afraid. Make the nervous butterflies fly in formation. If you can handle the potential outcome, act.

4. *In Failure, Give Up the Shame.* Grieve failures and wallow if you need to, but let go rather than absorb shame, and deflect

shame coming at you from others. Find new words to define a poor outcome.

5. *Failure Gives a Choice.* We don't always learn from failure; it is not a prerequisite for success. Many times it has nothing more to teach us than to examine the process and outcomes. It provides an escape hatch to find a different choice.

6. *More Effective Risk Taking.* Improve your decision making by examining the risks. Take only the risks you want, and avoid the ones that could prove fatal. What are the possible failures? What are the possible rewards? Is the reward worth the risk? Do I know the answer to that? Who else can help me?

7. *Process Trumps Outcome.* We are too focused on the binary outcome: success or failure. Business is all about cycles, and we need to focus on the process more than the outcome for better decision making that will improve our chance of success.

8. *Setting Patient Goals for Success and Failure.* Reality eventually collides with the dream that has been thrust upon us by others. Create your own dreams. Set goals before you start so you know what success and failure look like when you get there.

9. *A Measurement System of Our Own.* Money does not buy happiness. With what, besides money, will you measure your success?

10. *Value Action.* Stop reading this book and see what comes next. Experience builds confidence.

Biographies of Featured Less-Than-Famous Businesspeople

I have met many of the people featured in this book by kismet. Similar people are all around you. For the most part they are not famous and may never be. This fact is irrelevant. What is important is that they are more like us than anyone you'll ever read about in the everyday business press. Thank you to each one of them for sharing their lives so we can all learn.

Collin Anderson

I met Collin, an alumnus of the University of Chicago, at a New Venture Challenge judging panel. Unlike me, when he spoke, he was always able to articulate his thoughts perfectly. This is amazing considering he is the first person I have met from Montana.

Collin is an entrepreneur, small business consultant, inventor, and occasional unpaid teacher who has made a career of bridging the gap between invention and the marketplace. He is president and co-leader of Neuros and co-founder and past president/CEO of Digital

Innovations, both manufacturers of branded consumer electronics products. He previously worked in positions involving early-stage technology marketing, engineering project management, scientific research, and small business consulting.

Anna Belyaev

Anna is one of the most unique people I have met. Her background surely has shaped who she is and the way she views life.

Anna is founder and CEO of Type A Learning Agency (www .typea.net), an innovative consultancy that helps organizations drive change from the inside out. A recognized industry leader, Anna is frequently consulted about business and technology trends by parties as diverse as the Italian Trade Commission and the Canadian Department of Economic Development. She graduated magna cum laude, Phi Beta Kappa, from Lawrence University with a B.A. in Slavic languages and literature, and earned an M.A. in Russian literature and history from the University of Wisconsin–Madison. She has been actively involved in the development and application of learning technologies for nearly 20 years, having gotten her start at the National Center for Supercomputing Applications (NCSA) in the group that produced Telnet, Spyglass, and Netscape.

Brett Farmiloe

I met Brett Farmiloe by e-mail. I am glad his message did not go to spam. I was immediately taken by his idea to travel around the country and talk to people about pursuing their passion. In the summer of 2006, I helped sponsor his journey.

Brett graduated with a bachelor's degree in accounting from the University of Arizona in May 2006. Upon graduation he and two other students traveled over 10,000 miles to interview 100 individuals on the "Pursue the Passion" tour to learn about key characteristics of passionate people. Brett chronicled his experiences and interviews on the web site, PursuethePassion.com. He has launched another

14,000-mile journey in 2007 to continue to inspire students and adults to do what they want in life.

John Follis

John Follis is from New York and he embodies resiliency. As John puts it, he has been to the White House and the poor house.

One of 12 "Best of New York," as named by the Advertising Club of New York, John's work has been pronounced "simple and effective." His agency's campaigns have received press in the *New York Times, Wall Street Journal, USA Today, Time,* and *Forbes.* Besides receiving dozens of awards, John's work is highly effective. Six Follis campaigns are featured in college textbooks while another is a Harvard Business School case study.

Before starting Follis LLC, John was with several top U.S. agencies including DDB, K&B, and his own, Follis DeVito Verdi, one of Madison Avenue's most award-winning agencies. John is a contributing columnist for *Adweek* and author of a 2005 booklet, "How to Attract and Excite Your Prospects." A business owner since 1986, John is President of Follis LLC, which offers marketing therapy for businesses with limited budgets.

Will Harris

I met Will Harris at an agriculture conference I spoke at in Nashville. I am from the North and he is from the South. We could barely understand each other.

Will is a full-time cattleman in rural Georgia. His family has raised cattle on the same farm for 140 years, and his daughters are the fifth generation to do so. His land, his family, and his herd comprise what is important to Will, and they are his religion. Will learned the scientific way of raising cattle while majoring in animal science at the University of Georgia. He learned to administer artificial hormone implants, confinement-feed unnaturally high carbohydrate diets, utilize subcutaneous levels of antibiotics, and to use many of the other tools of the industrialized meat production system. He has since returned to the stockman approach that he learned from his father and grandfather and now produces White Oak Pastures all-natural grass-fed beef.

Deborah House

There is no one more fun to have lunch with than Deborah House. Her enthusiasm makes it hard for her to finish her meal. It is a good thing that I eat slowly.

As the CEO of The Adare Group, a strategy and profitability consulting firm, Deborah has been working with CEOs to maximize the profitability of Fortune 100 companies since 1981. She distinguishes herself by increasing company profits by record amounts. This is achieved through the dissection and examination of external forces, rather than indiscriminate expense reduction, and she has obtained tens of millions of dollars in financing for growing businesses. A CPA, Ms. House brings a wealth of experience from numerous financial executive positions including McDonald's Corporation, Amoco Corporation, GATX, and Fifth-Third Bank, where she was responsible for ensuring key financial results.

Mark Jepsen

As a video editor, Mark's office is a regular carnival with sights and sounds assaulting your senses.

Mark started his professional career 15 years ago when he left Columbia College a semester early to take his first editing job. His first assignment was a television commercial for a local celebrity-owned restaurant. When he saw that spot on the air, he was hooked. Since then, he's cut just about anything imaginable, from sales and training videos to sports shows and promos, but his first love and passion has always been cutting TV spots.

In 1997 he was editing for a regional sports network and had just won an Emmy for that work, when a friend who was also a creative director at FCB Chicago convinced him that his reel was so good that it could get him work at a commercial post production house. With that vote of confidence, he set out to Michigan Avenue, reel in hand. He landed at Swell in 1998, where he built a reputation as an editor with timing, style, and an ability to find the true humor in a comedy spot. He caught the eye of Luiz Landgraf at Machete. Mark could tell there was something special about what Luiz and his partners are building at Machete, and he now offers his creative talents as part of that dynamic team.

Colin Jones

I met Colin in the summer of 2006 when I visited Australia and spoke to his class at the University of Tasmania (UTAS). All my friends wanted a UTAS T-shirt. He had been using my first book as a text in his entrepreneurship class. Colin showed me Tassie hospitality. He has been a huge supporter of mine in the international education community.

The founder of many service-based, import-based, and education-related businesses, Colin has experienced the highs and lows of self-employment. A willingness to trust and assist others has helped to advance his life. Now a lecturer in entrepreneurship at the University of Tasmania, Colin continues to mentor local start-ups and his students. He was the 2005 winner of the Australian University Teaching Award. His career change has afforded Colin valuable reflection space within which to contemplate past failures and plan new entrepreneurial ventures. He is now developing a consultancy practice focused on creative problem-solving and educational leadership, which offers him a new direction for his future energies.

Scott Jordan

Not too many lawyers can start a company and become an innovative businessperson. Scott is one of those few. I assisted him in the early years of Scottevest (SeV), but he quickly outpaced my skills. Now he runs a multimillion-dollar empire from Ketchum, Idaho.

Scott is the founder and CEO of SeV. Before founding the company, Scott practiced real estate and corporate law. Scott received his J.D. degree from Case Western Reserve University College of Law in May 1992. But the law bored Scott; he was always an entrepreneur at heart. As a result of Scott's accomplishments with SeV, he has been written about extensively, including several articles in the *Wall Street Journal* and *New York Times* and several college textbooks. Scott has since been featured in many TV shows, including the hit show *Radical Sabbatical* as well as Japan's hit show *The World's Most Successful People*.

Andria Lieu

Fashion designer Andria Lieu was born in Vietnam, the youngest of five children. At the age of 12, she and her family were forced to flee their homeland during the North Vietnamese takeover. They arrived at a refugee camp on an island in Malaysia where they awaited sponsorship to immigrate to a new home. Andria's family received an invitation from a small town in Michigan where they then settled.

The summer before attending college, Andria enrolled in a fashion illustration class at the Art Institute of Chicago. There her instructor recognized her talent and persuaded her to enroll in the bachelor's degree program for fashion design. Upon completion of the program, Andrea entered her designs in New York's NAMSB competition and won the prestigious Best Menswear Designer award. This won her the attention of a Chicago-based menswear manufacturer who hired Andria to design men's clothing and accessories. She soon realized her desire to develop her own collection of women's wear and began working nights creating the Andria Lieu Collection. Designing, manufacturing, and selling her own line, she eventually left her position with the menswear company to grow her own successful business.

Jing Ma

I met Jing at a presentation on a Saturday morning in Maryland. I was immediately impressed with her drive and fortitude to achieve what she wanted.

Having came here from China, Jing Ma has the dream of going back there as an influential politician. She started out as a youth in the Junior Mao Party. Jing later realized the benefits of capitalism when her father was successful in creating a product for the railroad industry. He was named as one of the 100 most important people in China for his contribution. She is currently at KPMG as a senior associate in the technology, communication, and entertainment area. She has managed due diligence for Fortune 500 clients.

Rick Mazursky

Rick is my business mentor. He brings me back into the sailboat when I fall overboard and lose my way.

He has over 35 years of experience in retail and consumer products. specifically in product design, marketing, merchandising, and all forms of domestic and international distribution, particularly to the mass market. Rick also has extensive hands-on knowledge of product development and manufacturing in the Far East. Rick has had leadership positions in a number of companies involved in the creation and distribution of consumer products including electronic educational toys, consumer electronics, and software. He was involved in the launching of Cabbage Patch Dolls, was a partner in a toy company sold to a public company, and served as president of VTech Toys and CEO of Digital Innovations. When designing a product line, Rick always tells me that whatever we sell has to "look like they all got dressed in the same room."

Matt McCall

Matthew McCall is a co-founder and managing director of Portage Venture Partners and the newer Draper Fisher Jurvetson Portage Venture Partners. In recent years, when I am unable to figure out a complex business situation, I visit Matt. He talks. I listen. I write. I rely on his wisdom. I frequently read his popular venture blog called VC Confidential. He recently sold one of his companies, Feedburner, to Google.

Matt has served on the advisory board to the Mayor's Council of Technology Advisors in Chicago as well as on numerous other regional high-technology advisory boards. He is a board member of the Illinois Venture Capital Association. He has been honored by Crain's *Chicago Business* on its annual "40 under 40" list of leading Chicagoans under age 40. He has also been named as one of the 100 most prominent members of Chicago's technology community. He has keynoted or been a panelist at over 50 area conferences and events nationwide.

Nick Papadopoulos

Selling is a critical skill in business. Without sales, we have no customers. Without customers, we only have a hobby. When I have a sales question, I call Coach Nick.

Nicholas Papadopoulos is the founder of Championship Selling, a methodology that helps sales organizations, executives, and professionals gain confidence by developing smart sales plans. Coach Nick is the author of the sales book *Coach Nick's Championship Selling,* a Quick Guide book (Martin Training Associates, 2005). Nick has 20 years of experience both integrating and improving multiple sales channels within large organizations as well as managing the sales function at key start-ups. The Coach inspires sales organizations to create a truly winning environment by recommending more effective organizational structures, helping to identify and hire the right people, and providing input on ways to make sales and marketing teams more collaborative and productive.

Linda Regulbuto

I met Linda when I spoke at a Community Wealth Ventures conference where they teach nonprofits how to start for-profit subsidiaries to support their organization. I was immediately impressed by Linda's life experience. She refers to herself as "an adult child of entrepreneurs," is married to an entrepreneur, and has recently discovered that her young daughter is following the family tradition.

Linda is the education and community relations manager for the Bushnell Center for the Performing Arts in Hartford, Connecticut, where she enthusiastically develops new business ventures, community initiatives, and audience development programs. She joined the Bushnell after 22 years as owner, director, and administrator of two successful businesses in Connecticut. Her background in educational and elder services research and experience led to the development of three instructional and motivational videotapes for the geriatric market, and master classes and seminars for the National Association of Dance and Affiliated Artists. Linda has appeared on several TV, cable, and radio programs and served on the board of advisers for Dance Services Network Seniors Programs, *Bravo Newspaper* Senior Sector, and is a former choreographer for the Macy's Thanksgiving Day Parade!

Larry Terkel

I met Larry at a National Speakers Conference. His business card says that he is an author and speaker, businessman and minister, and yoga and meditation teacher. That's a lot for one person, but Larry is familiar with unusual paths. He was born Methodist, adopted and raised by a Jewish family, then found his birth mother and learned he was part Scotch Irish and part Cherokee Indian.

After graduation from Cornell University in 1970, where Larry earned a B.S. and an M.B.A., he and his new wife, Susan, traveled for one year and studied Hinduism, Buddhism, and yoga in India. When they returned to the United States, Larry earned an M.A. in philosophy and comparative religion from Kent State University. In 1995 he served as CEO of a public company and in 1996 founded Global Health Care, Inc., a distributor of rapid biomedical diagnostics with offices in the USA and Mexico.

In 1978, Larry and Susan bought an old church on the town square of Hudson, Ohio. They founded the Spiritual Life Society, an inter-denominational center for spiritual and holistic studies. As its licensed minister, Larry has officiated at over 2,000 weddings for couples of all faiths. Larry is also the co-author of *Small Change: It's the LITTLE Things in Life That Make a BIG Difference!* (Tarcher, 2004) which was a finalist for the 2004 National Books for a Better Life Award.

Kara Trott

I met Kara when we spoke on the same program for the Federal Reserve Bank. Kara Trott is CEO and founder of Quantum Health, a health benefits plan management firm located in Columbus, Ohio. Quantum Health operates Coordinated Health/Care, a program that has successfully contained participating employers' health care costs to a 5–6 percent trend over the past six years, with no reduction in benefits or cost sharing—about one-third the national average. Under Kara's leadership, Quantum Health has seen approximately 30 to 40 percent annual growth and now operates in more than 40 health plans around the country.

Kara is an active member of Women Presidents' Organization, the National Association of Women Business Owners, and the Buckeye Gazelles Association and is on the advisory board for both Key4Women (KeyBank) and Enterprising Women.

Bruce Zamost

I met Bruce in 1977 as a college freshman at Brandeis University. At the time, he embodied *cool* to me. Each of us began our respec-tive undergraduate careers as liberal arts generalists, me as a political science major, Bruce as a philosophy major. What I admire most about Bruce is his self-assured disposition. For example, when his girlfriend and I enrolled in the est Training seminars, he steadfastly declined our invitation to join us. He politely attended the est pitch and promptly advised that he would instead be investing his $300 registration fee in a leather jacket.

Bruce has applied that confidence to his 22-year career as a product liability attorney, representing victims of defective industrial machinery, consumer tools, and other products. Beneath his trial lawyer's garb, I suspect that Bruce's success in the courtroom is, in part, attributable to that invisible leather jacket he wears under his skin. Bruce's efforts in product liability law culminated in 2000 with the publication of the New Jersey Supreme Court's decision in *Cavanaugh v. Skil Corporation*. Bruce is a shareholder with Stark & Stark. In 2004, *SJ Magazine* named Bruce its top product liability attorney in South Jersey.

Notes

Chapter 1 Get Ready for Adventure

1. David Myers, *The Pursuit of Happiness* (Harper, 1993), information at http://www.davidmyers.org/Brix?pageID=48.

2. DJ Clawson's Underdog web site is at http://www.geocities.com/SoHo/8850/udog.htm.

3. For the official way to make a rubber band ball, see www.wikihow.com/Make-a-Rubber-Band-Ball.

Chapter 2 Archetypes of Success

1. http://www.financial-freedom-made-simple.com/Motivational-Quotes.html.

2. http://www.financial-freedom-made-simple.com/Motivational-Quotes.html.

3. University of California Regents, http://ucsfhr.ucsf.edu/hrupdate/update200202.htm.

4. At a speech in September 2006, U.S. Small Business Development Conference, Houston, Texas.

5. An archetype is defined as "the original pattern or model from which all things of the same kind are copied or on which they are based; a model or first form; prototype" (http://dictionary.reference.com/browse/archetype).

6. Jonathan Black, *Yes You Can!* (Bloomsbury, 2006), 121.

7. Combined statistics from various university web sites including Indiana University, University of Pennsylvania, and Yale.

8. With 7.5 million millionaires in the United States as of 2004, this represents about 2.5 percent of the population.

9. *Stuff* magazine, December 2006.

10. Joey Green, *The Road to Success is Paved with Failure* (Little, Brown and Company, 2001).

11. "*Publishers Weekly* declared Grisham 'the bestselling novelist of the 90s,' selling a total of 60,742,289 copies. He is also one of only two authors to sell two million copies on a first printing (Tom Clancy is the other). Grisham's 1992 novel *The Pelican Brief* sold 11,232,480 copies in the United States alone." http://en.wikipedia.org/wiki/John_Grisham.

12. http://en.wikipedia.org/wiki/Simon_Cowell.

13. http://news.bbc.co.uk/1/hi/uk/2979033.stm.

14. Chip and Dan Heath, "The Myth about Creation Myths," *Fast Company*, March 2007. In the same article, the authors talk about how Apple's Jobs and Wozniak got their start at Atari and Hewlett Packard.

15. David Guggenheim, director, quoting Twain in the film *The Inconvenient Truth,* 2005.

16. Consider the case of Ken Lay of Enron, who died of a heart attack. Some say he paid the ultimate price. Others say he escaped justice.

17. http://hbswk.hbs.edu/archive/4367.html.

18. *American Way,* December 1, 2006, 70.

19. Ibid.

20. http://en.wikipedia.org/wiki/Malcolm_Bricklin.

Chapter 3 *I Have Got Your One-Hit Wonder*

1. The name *Wonders* was originally spelled "One-ders," a deliberate play on the term. Ironically, while the movie was in theaters, the soundtrack got only as high as number 26 on the charts. The Wonders never made it to the charts again, so they were, in a sense, both a real and fictitious one-hit wonder band. http://en.wikipedia.org/wiki/One-hit_wonder.

2. Mark Cuban's blog is at http://www.blogmaverick.com/2005/05/30/success-and-motivation-you-only-have-to-be-right-once/.

3. http://www.brainyquote.com/quotes/authors/w/wayne_gretzky.html.

Chapter 4 *The World from Here*

1. http://www.quotulatiousness.ca/d.html.

2. *Schadenfreude* is defined as "satisfaction or pleasure felt at someone else's misfortune." (www.dictionary.com)

3. Paper written by Jill Kickul students, 14. Kickul is the Forsythe Chair in Entrepreneurship at the Thomas C. Page Center for Entrepreneurship Richard T. Farmer School of Business Miami University. In 2004, she had her students help do basic research and interviews for this book.

4. Daniel McGinn, "The Trouble with Lifestyle Entrepreneurs,"*Inc,* July 2005, http://www.inc.com/magazine/20050701/business-culture.html.

5. Johan Wiklund, "Business Failure: Fatal Blow or Learning Experience?" Presented at the "Fail Forward, Is Failure Victory?" seminar in Brussels, Belgium, November 9, 2005.

6. Paper written by Jill Kickul students, 14.

7. GEM 2005 Executive Report, http://www.gemconsortium.org/document. aspx?id=448, page 23.

8. www.natlaw.com/pubs/spchbr1.htm.

9. http://news.bbc.co.uk/2/hi/business/5291910.stm.

10. World Bank statistics taken from http://www.doingbusiness.org/ExploreTopics/ ClosingBusiness/. The Doing. Business database provides objective measures of business regulations and their enforcement. The indicators are comparable across 175 economies. They indicate the regulatory costs of business and can be used to analyze specific regulations that enhance or constrain investment, productivity, and growth.

Chapter 5 *Forget the Archetypes*

1. According to Wikipedia, the expression derives from *umble pie,* which was a pie filled with liver, heart, and other offal, especially of cow but often deer. These parts were known as *umbles,* and since they were considered inferior food, in medieval times the pie was often served to lower-class people. It was almost as undesirable as eating crow.

2. http://dictionary.reference.com/browse/humility.

3. http://www.investopedia.com/university/concepts/concepts5.asp#.

4. Jeffrey Rosenthal, *Struck by Lightning* (Joseph Henry Press, 2006).

5. Barry Moltz, *You Need to Be a Little Crazy* (Kaplan Publishing, 2003), 45.

6. Dean Koontz, *Mr. Murder* (Berkley, 2006).

7. http://en.wikipedia.org/wiki/Hubris. Aristotle defined hubris as "Doing or saying things that cause shame to the victim, not in order that anything may happen to you, nor because anything has happened to you, but merely for your own gratification. Hubris is not the requital of past injuries; this is revenge. As for the pleasure in hubris, its cause is this: men think that by ill-treating others they make their own superiority the greater."

8. Sang Hoon Nam, "Culture and Managerial Responses to Failure: A Comparison Between Korea and the USA," University of Victoria, Written for the International Industrial Relations Association in 2004.

9. If Michael Dell had kept the original name of the company PC's Limited, the business may not have been as successful.

10. Bo Peabody, *Lucky or Smart? Secrets to an Entrepreneurial Life* (Random House, 2004).

11. Ibid.

12. http://en.wikipedia.org/wiki/Ego_the_Living_Planet.

13. http://en.wikipedia.org/wiki/Ego%2C_super-ego%2C_and_id.

14. Lea Strickland, "Is Ego the Problem?" *Carolina Newswire,* August 2, 2005.

15. Peabody, *Lucky or Smart?*

16. Paul Stiles, *Is the American Dream Killing You? How "The Market" Rules Our Lives* (Harper Collins, 2005), 192.

17. GEM 2005 Executive Report.

18. Thea Singer, "Our Companies, Ourselves," *Inc,* November 2006, 39.

19. Ibid, 40.

20. Ibid.

21. David Freedman, "What's Next: Mistakes Were Made", *Inc.,* October 2006. http://www.inc.com/magazine/20061001/column-freedman.html

22. The Tylenol Crisis, http://www.aerobiologicalengineering.com/wxk116/TylenolMurders/crisis.html

23. http://www.mallenbaker.net/csr/CSRfiles/crisis02.html.

24. Market capitalization as of July 2007.

25. Tamara Kaplan, "The Tylenol Crisis: How Effective Public Relations Saved Johnson & Johnson," http://www.aerobiologicalengineering.com/wxk116/TylenolMurders/crisis.html

Chapter 6 Failure Is an Option

1. Larry Farrell, *Across the Board*, September 2005.

2. Jeremy Gangemi, "Starting Over When Your Business Fails," *BusinessWeek,* August 2006.

3. Speech at fund-raising luncheon in Chicago, October 2006.

4. Jill Kickul student papers. Kickul is the Forsythe Chair in Entrepreneurship at the Thomas C. Page Center for Entrepreneurship Richard T. Farmer School

of Business Miami University. In 2004, she had her students help do basic research and interviews for this book.

5. Alan Webber, "Is Your Next Job Calling You?" *Fast Company,* January 1998.

6. www.escapefromcubiclenation.com

7. Joshua Piven, *As Luck Would Have It: Incredible Stories from Lottery Wins to Lightning Strikes* (Villard, 2003).

Chapter 7 Embracing Failure When It Happens

1. Jill Kickul student research paper. Kickul is the Forsythe Chair in Entrepreneurship at the Thomas C. Page Center for Entrepreneurship Richard T. Farmer School of Business Miami University. In 2004, she had her students help do basic research and interviews for this book.

Chapter 8 Failure Provides Choices

1. http://www.teamfca.net/national/TEAMFCA/TheCompetitorsCreed.lsp

2. Mary Schmich, *Chicago Tribune,* November 2006.

3. Hesh Reinfeld, "Revel in Your Accomplishments; Don't Dwell on Missed Opportunities," 2006 http://www.heshreinfeld.com/columns.html

4. Ibid.

5. Head of Dept. of Economics, UC Berkeley, to 1996 economics graduatess at their commencement. http://www.ncsa.uiuc.edu/~fbaker/OTDs.html.

6. Jeff Wuorio, "How Business Failure Paves the Way to Success," http://www .microsoft.com/smallbusiness/resources/management/leadership_training/ how_business_failure_paves_the_way_to_success.mspx.

7. Ian Wylie, "Failure is Glorious," *Fast Company,* September 2001.

8. Name changed for anonymity.

9. Evan Schwartz, "What Steve Wozniak Learned from Failure," Harvard Business School's *Working Knowledge,* September 13, 2004, http://hbswk.hbs.edu/archive/ 4367.html.

10. Details about this annual tour are at www.pursuethepassion.com. I was a sponsor for the initial trip in 2006.

11. Ellen Byron, "Speaking of Success," *Wall Street Journal,* July 12, 2004, R-10.

12. Joseph Weber and Louis Lavelle et al, "Family, Inc." *BusinessWeek,* November 10, 2003.

13. Rod Kurtz, "Failure is Part of Success," *BusinessWeek Online,* June 22, 2005.

Chapter 9 Do It Anyway

1. My friend never took possession of the car but from then on, he kidded me that he let me drive "his" automobile.

2. The win-the-lottery dream can also be the "antiques road show" dream where the lucky person discovers that the dusty black-and-white rug folded in the attic corner just happens to be an original Navajo blanket that could fetch $400,000 or more at auction. The biggest systematic business windfall example of our times is probably the Internet bubble of the late 1990s, where millions were made as investors rode the American stock market up to historic heights (many also rode it down to new lows).

3. Source: Certified Financial Planner Board of Standards, Inc, http://www.cfp.net.

4. Gail Blanke, *Between Trapezes: Flying into a New Life with the Greatest of Ease* (Rodale Books, 2004).

5. Ibid.

Chapter 10 A Little DAB Will Do Ya!ⁱ

i. The popular marketing slogan for Brylcreem in the 1946.

1. Gregory Dibb, "A Study of the Mighty Motors Operating System: Making Sustainable Improvements at a Powertrain Manufacturing Facility," MIT, June 2004.

2. *The Consilient Observer,* Credit Suisse First Boston, October 7, 2003.

3. Michael Crichton also uses this as an opening to his book *Next* (HarperTorch, 2007).

4. Interview on the Oprah Winfrey show, November 15, 2006.

5. David Freedman, "Do You Manage By the Numbers?" *Inc,* November 2006, 60.

6. "I worked with Beth's mother, Liz a few years back in a new business venture. Suddenly, she had to leave to take care of her daughter, Beth, whose stove exploded as a result of a gas leak in her kitchen."

7. *The Consilient Observer,* Credit Suisse First Boston, October 7, 2003.

8. J. Edward Russo and Paul Schoemaker, *Winning Decisions* (New York: Doubleday, 2002).

9. *The Consilient Observer,* Credit Suisse First Boston, October 7, 2003.

10. If I hate to fly, how could I sail? Yes, I get seasick. Thanks to Marty Bernstein at Machete and Brian Briggs at Mission Expert for educating me in this area.

11. Amanda Kooser, "Burning Bright," *Entrepreneur,* August 2006.

Chapter 11 Goal Setting

1. http://www.quotedb.com/speeches/to-the-moon

2. The Schwab Center for Investment Research is part of Charles Schwab & Co., Inc., April 2006.

3. David Myers, "Wealth, Well-Being, and the New American Dream"http://www.davidmyers.org/Brix?pageID=49

4. Nitzan Danit, "Working Out: Not Just for the Holiday Resolutions" October 9, 2006 http://www.haaretz.com/hasen/spages/772028.html

5. Associated Press, "YMCAs Offer Customized Workout Programs," June 27, 2005 http://www.msnbc.msn.com/id/8373791/

6. At Eslide, **a graphic design company that specializes in professional quality presentations**, they refer to this type of work as "NIN" (*need it now*) because their clients deadlines are always so tight.

7. Studies from the University of Utah show that a person talking on the phone while driving (hands free or not) shows the same impaired reaction level as someone who is legally drunk in many states.

8. Peter Ferenczi, "Brain Strain,"*Laptop Magazine,* November 2006, 94.

9. Ibid.

10. Erika Schickel, "Stuggling to Create the Best Kids on the Block,"*Chicago Tribune,* September 24, 2006, Book Section 10. The full quote is "Boredom is the dream bird that hatches the egg of experience. A rustling in the leaves drives him away."

11. The position for seated zazen is with folded legs and hands, and an erect spine.

12. VC Confidential Blog, "Just Showing Up," October 31, 2006, http://www.vcconfidential.com/2006/10/just_showing_up.html.

13. Black, *Yes You Can!* 125.

14. http://www.brainyquote.com/quotes/authors/s/steven_wright.html.

Chapter 12 No Longer Black and White

1. Ellen Lee, "Jobs Knew of Apple Stock Options Practice,"*San Francisco Chronicle,* October 4, 2006.

2. Associated Press, "Two Executives at Japanese Firm to Resign in Accounting Scandal,"*New York Times,* December 26, 2006.

3. Stiles, *Is the American Dream Killing You?* 106–107

4. Martha Irvine, "U.S. Youth Priority," Chicago Tribune, January 23, 2007.

5. David Freedman, "Do You Manage By the Numbers?"*Inc,* November 2006, 60.

6. David Myers, "The Third Culture"http://www.edge.org/3rd_culture/story/54.html

7. Ibid.

8. Jonathan Black, *Yes You Can!* 122.

9. Ibid., 123.

10. For comparison, the savings rate in Japan is13 percent; in Germany, 12 percent; and in France, 15 percent.

11. Stiles, *Is the American Dream Killing You?* 33.

12. Ibid., 225.

13. Ibid., 226.

14. David Myers, The Third Culture http://www.edge.org/3rd_culture/story/54.html

15. Ibid.

16. Ibid. The humor of this is based on the phrase, "The economy, stupid," coined by James Carville and used during Bill Clinton's 1992 presidential campaign against George Bush Sr. The phrase became catchy in American politics, and has been since modified for a multitude of purposes—"It's the , stupid."

17. Erika Schickel, "Struggling to Create the Best Kids on the Block," *Chicago Tribune,* September 24, 2006.

18. Daniel McGinn, "The Trouble with Lifestyle Entrepreneurs," *Inc,* July 2005.

19. Ibid.

20. *Journal of Personality and Social Psychology,* published by the American Psychological Association (APA), February 2001.

21. Bo Burlingham, "Small Is the New Big," *Inc,* February 2006.

22. Ibid.

Chapter 13 Read This Book—Then Throw It Away

1. Gwen Moran and Sue Johnson, *The Complete Idiot's Guide to Business Plans* (Alpha Books, 2005), Foreword.

2. A quote Michael Crichton uses at the beginning of his book *Next* (HarperTorch, 2007).

3. http://www.quotationspage.com/quote/3141.html.

4. As I remember from high school and early college, these text commands were entered on a screen or on a paper teletype machine.

5. Rick Adams, The Colossal Cave, www.rickadams.org/adventure/d_hints/index.html.

Index